More Frontier Justice
in the Wild West

MORE FRONTIER JUSTICE IN THE WILD WEST

Bungled, Bizarre, and Fascinating Executions

R. MICHAEL WILSON

Guilford, Connecticut
Helena, Montana
An imprint of Rowman & Littlefield

A · TWODOT® · BOOK

Distributed by NATIONAL BOOK NETWORK

Copyright © 2014 by R. Michael Wilson

TwoDot is a registered trademark of Rowman & Littlefield

British Library Cataloguing-in-Publication Information available

Library of Congress Cataloging-in-Publication Data available

ISBN 978-0-7627-9602-1 (paperback)

The paper used in this publication meets the minimum requirements of American National Standard for Information Sciences—Permanence of Paper for Printed Library Materials, ANSI/ NISO Z39.48-1992.

Contents

INTRODUCTION

The administration of justice on America's western frontier was relatively consistent. Even when citizens resorted to vigilante action, a sentence of death was usually restricted to situations where a premeditated, cold-blooded murder had been proven, or at least proven to the majority of the mob. There were a few exceptions among extralegal executions, and many lynchings went unreported or unconfirmed, but among the numerous legal executions occurring before the end of 1911 there was only one man hanged for a crime other than first-degree murder: Thomas Ketchum. He was hanged in Clayton County, New Mexico, for assaulting a train, and his execution was among several of the most bungled affairs in the annals of the Old West. However, the decapitation of Thomas Ketchum was not the only bungled execution in the West.

Pablita Sandoval, one of only two women executed on the western frontier, met Miguel Martin when she was twenty-six years old, and a torrid affair followed. Martin, husband and father of five, soon tired of the relationship with his mistress and informed her that he wanted to end things, but Sandoval convinced Martin to see her one last time. On March 23, 1861, they met; Sandoval hugged her lover for the last time, and while Martin was distracted, she pulled a butcher knife from the folds of her dress and stabbed him to death. Sandoval was arrested, held over for trial, convicted of murder in the first degree, and sentenced to hang. Sheriff Antonio Herrera selected for the gallows a cottonwood tree within one mile of the Church of Las Vegas, New Mexico. At 10:00 a.m. on April 26, 1861, Sandoval was placed in a wagon, where she sat upon her coffin. Sheriff Herrera drove the wagon directly beneath the limb, ordered Sandoval to stand, and hurriedly adjusted the noose before he jumped onto the wagon seat and whipped up the horses. The wagon lurched forward from beneath Sandoval's feet before the sheriff realized he had not bound the condemned woman's wrists and ankles. Sandoval was strangling while struggling to pull herself up, so the sheriff used all his weight to pull down on her legs. Outraged spectators rushed in, pushed the sheriff away, and cut down Sandoval. Colonel J. D. Serna then read the death warrant, which stated clearly that Sandoval was to be "hanged until dead." The sheriff backed the team and wagon under the limb, tied a new noose in the rope, lifted Sandoval into the wagon bed and put the noose around her neck, and pinioned her wrists and ankles. He took but a moment to examine his work before driving the wagon out a second time, and the law was satisfied.

New Mexico, it seems, was the worst place to be executed. When William Wilson was hanged on December 10, 1875, he had the benefit of a gallows and a carefully calculated drop, but it did not improve his chances for a merciful death. The lever was kicked, the trapdoor sprung, and Wilson fell, but his neck was not broken. After nine and one-half minutes of strangling, the body went limp and then he was cut down without a doctor's examination. His remains were placed in a coffin, and the black hood was removed. Spectators were allowed to file past to have one last look at the murderer when one curious Mexican woman, making a careful examination of the body, suddenly cried out "For God's sake, the dead has come to life." Wilson was then examined by the attending physician and found to be alive. A rope was quickly tossed over the crossbeam of the scaffold, an impromptu noose was tied around Wilson's neck, and several men from the crowd pulled the condemned man right up out of his coffin. He hanged another twenty minutes until strangulation finally completed the task required by law.

Hanging remained the most common form of execution on the western frontier, and there were two basic forms of gallows. The most common scaffold was built with a platform about eight feet above the ground and the condemned man was dropped through a trapdoor. In about a quarter of the executions, the gallows was a platform at ground level and the rope was attached to a great weight suspended above the ground which, when dropped, jerked the man upward, breaking his neck. There are no recorded decapitations using a "twitch-up" gallows, but on December 27, 1889, Nah-diez-az, a very lightweight Pinal Indian, was jerked up so forcefully by a 340-pound copper ingot that his skull was crushed on the crossbeam. In Colorado this latter form of gallows was improved almost to perfection. It was called "the automatic suicide machine," because the weight of the condemned man on the platform activated the release. The act of "springing the trap" or "dropping the weight" was particularly disagreeable, so other means of doing so were adopted. Perhaps the most famous was the water lever release system used in Wyoming to hang teenager Charles Miller on April 22, 1892, and Tom Horn on November 20, 1903. Time and experience did not seem to improve hangings, and on November 10, 1916, Lucius Hightower was decapitated by a trapdoor gallows. In June 1890, in Nevada, Elizabeth Potts narrowly escaped beheading by the skin of her neck, but on February 21, 1930, Eva Dugan was decapitated in Arizona, and the outrage led to a legislative change to the use of the gas chamber.

A hanged man usually remained suspended until an attending physician pronounced him dead. The time varied with each individual, but one scientist who argued for electrocution as a substitute for hanging stated that, "a man is usually sixteen minutes dying at the end of a hangman's rope." In fact, every hanging was unique, and Dr. D. S. Lamb, an ex-surgeon of the United States Army, studied the subject and in 1894 reported in the *St. Louis Globe-Democrat:*

DEATH BY HANGING –
The Three Different Stages Through Which the Victim Passes

I have made the subject of death by hanging a long study. From my observations during my experience in the army I feel justified in saying that death by hanging is the most exaggerated of all modes. It may be immediate and without symptoms but the subject must pass through three stages before death.

In the first stage the victim passes into a partial stupor lasting from thirty seconds to two minutes, but this is generally governed by the length of the drop, the weight of the body, and the tightness of the constriction. There is absolutely no pain in this stage; the feeling is rather one of pleasure. The subjective symptoms described are intense heat in the head, brilliant flashes of light in the eyes, deafening sounds in the ears and a heavy numb feeling in the lungs. In the second stage the subject passes into unconsciousness and convulsions usually occur. In the third stage all is quiet except the beating of the heart. Just before death the agitation is renewed, but in a different way from that in the second state. The feet are raised, the tongue has a peculiar spasm, the chest heaves, the eyes protrude from the orbits and oscillate from side to side, and the pupils dilate. The pulse can, in most cases, be felt ten minutes after the drop.

I once knew a man who was desirous of ascertaining if there was any suffering by hanging and in order to find out he placed a rope around his neck and stepped off a bench, intending to step back again, but he became immediately unconscious and would have died in a few minutes had it not been for the timely arrival of a friend. He said he experienced all the feelings that I mentioned in the first stage.

This three stage process depended upon the noose being properly knotted and adjusted. The knot was carefully positioned on the left shoulder just behind the jaw so that it would press upon the carotid artery cutting off blood to the brain, which resulted in unconsciousness in a few seconds. This positioning of the knot forced the head to snap back and resulted in a "broken neck." Ideally, during a legal hanging, the spine would be dislocated between the first and second or the second and third cervical vertebrae and the spinal cord would be severed, or at least severely compressed, cutting off all sensation to the torso and extremities. One of the main criticisms of hanging as a means of execution was that the condemned man's neck was, all too often, unbroken and he would "perish by the long and painful process of strangulation." John Burns, however, spoke from personal experience in refuting that perception. He reported, "Some time during the war ruffians, who desired to be thought (bush) whackers, came upon me at my house, intending to compel me to give up some money I was supposed to have. I had none, and told them so, but they did not believe me and their next move was to cut a cord out of a bedstead, tie one end around my neck, throw the other over a joist overhead, and pull me up till my feet were clear of the floor. This they did four times, questioning me between whiles. I lost consciousness every time as soon as my feet left the floor but felt no pain at any time, and after the second hoist I meant to sham continued insensibility when they let me drop again, since to lower me they just let go the rope and I fell to the floor, but this was beyond my power. My first consciousness was that I had raised my body to a sitting position, which put shamming out of the question. I experienced no pain when the rope tightened, nor when I was suspended, nor after I was released, except the soreness caused on my skin by the chafing of the rope. I weighed about two hundred pounds, which insured that the rope was fully tightened each time.

Hanging was not the only means of execution on America's western frontier, and the alternative of being shot by a firing squad could also be bungled. In Utah in 1879 a condemned murderer had his choice of being hanged, shot, or beheaded. Wallace Wilkerson elected to be shot on May 16, 1879, and his last request was that his eyes remain uncovered and his hands free. The prisoner was escorted to a chair in the jail yard and a paper target was pinned over his heart. After Wilkerson sat down he called out loudly, "Aim for my heart, Marshal!" At a given signal the rifles were put through portholes, and at a second signal the rifles steadied their aim on the paper target. The moment was tense for everyone, but especially for Wilkerson. When the second signal was heard, the condemned man, in anticipation of the gunshots, suddenly straightened in his chair, threw his chest forward, and raised his head erect, which had the effect of raising the paper target more than an inch. The rifles then steadied their aim on the raised target, and it was but a moment before the third signal was given and the rifles discharged. Three leaden balls struck the paper target precisely. The condemned man stood, turned to the south, pitched forward two steps, and fell, as all three bullets had struck above his heart. As he lay on the ground, he turned his head to look up and cried out, "My God! My God! They missed it!" He lay there, groaning and gasping for breath while the attending physicians hurried to the dying man. They stayed with him until all signs of life were stilled, which took fifteen minutes, and they reported that he was wholly conscious and clearly demonstrated sensation until seconds before his death. Officials were relieved when he was pronounced dead, as they had been considering shooting him again while he lay on the ground suffering. In response to the horror and brutality of Wilkerson's execution, the May 17 edition of the *Daily Ogden Junction* issued an editorial in support of the guillotine:

The execution of Wallace Wilkerson at Provo yesterday affords another illustration of the brutal exhibitions of inquisitorial torture that have of late disgraced the country and which have in some states so shocked the natural sensibilities of the people that extreme punishment has been abrogated from pure disgust excited by the sickening spectacles of rotten ropes, ignorantly or carelessly adjusted nooses or inexperienced marksmen. These disgusting scenes are invariably ascribed to accidental causes, but they have become so horrifyingly frequent that some other method of judicial murder should be adopted. The French Guillotine never fails. The swift falling knife flashes in the light, a dull thud is heard and all is over. It is eminently more merciful to the victim than our bungling atrocities, and the ends of justice are as fully secured.

With the choice left to the condemned man, however, it should be no surprise that beheading was never selected, and this means of execution in Utah was removed as an alternative in 1888. The outrage at the execution of Wilkerson might have been misplaced, as there were eleven men shot to death in Utah and his was the only bungled affair. The "disgusting scene" was the result of granting the man's last wish that he not be blindfolded and restrained and the result of his response to the signals, and could not be attributed to any error on the part of officials. In the case of shooting, the firing squad usually consisted of from three to nine "crack" marksmen. Their weapons were rifles, except in the Indian Territory, where pistols at point-blank range were sometimes used. In most cases one or several rifles were loaded with powder only. This was an accommodation to the firing party, not only to steady their aim, but also so each man could later, if needed, rationalize his weapon was loaded with the blank. The distance to the target was usually thirty feet or less, and the executioners, hidden from view, had some apparatus to support their aim such as a bench or table.

M. Wall Espy and John O. Smykla compiled the ESPY File—a list of executions in the United States between 1608 and 2002. While the list is a good place to start an investigation into early American capital punishment, there are many omissions and more than a few extralegal executions sprinkled in to cloud the integrity of the list. However, according to the ESPY File, there were 1,125 executions on the western frontier before the end of 1910. In Oklahoma twenty-three of their forty-eight condemned men were shot; in Utah the count was ten of fourteen men executed by firing party; and in Texas four men were shot prior to August 1864. All the others, 1,085 men and 2 women listed, were hanged. The count by western state or territory follows:

Arizona	*39*
California	*264*
Colorado	*43*
Idaho	*21*
Kansas	*16*
Montana	*46*
Nebraska	*20*
Nevada	*29*
New Mexico	*47*
North Dakota	*8*
Oklahoma	*48*
Oregon	*79*
South Dakota	*13*
Texas	*230*
Utah	*14*
Washington	*46*
Wyoming	*8*

One other method of frontier justice existed—that of killing the criminal miscreant while in the commission of an unlawful act or while he was resisting arrest. The twenty chapters of frontier justice detailed on the following pages represent some of the most thrilling events in the effort to rid the western frontier of desperate men.

CHAPTER 1

A Soldier's Revenge

In 1874 elements of the 4th Cavalry and 19th Infantry were stationed at Fort Whipple in the Arizona Territory. In late March 1874, Private Edgar R. Maynard, alias Joseph K. Dunlap, assigned to Company B of the 4th Cavalry, broke into George Davidson's home, which was located within the fort. He stole jewelry and was soon arrested, charged with burglary, and lodged in the guardhouse. He was scheduled to receive a general court-martial on March 30, 1874. The board was assigned on March 29 and included Major D. L. Magruder, Captains M. P. Small and R. P. Wilson, and Lieutenants G. A. Goodale, Charles Bird, and D. L. Weiting. They heard the evidence over the next two days, including the testimony of Corporal Richard L. Lawler, then adjourned without publishing their findings or sentence. On April 17 Prescott's *Miner* published both:

> *The following has reference to a wicked soldier who, on a recent evening, broke into the dwelling of Mr. Geo. Davidson, at Fort Whipple, and stole therefrom, jewelry of considerable value.*
>
> *Private Edgar R. Maynard, alias Joseph K. Dunlap, Company B, 4th Infantry* (sic).
>
> *ne Specification.*
>
> *Plea—not guilty.*
>
> *Finding—guilty.*

Sentence—"To forfeit all pay and allowances that are now due or that may become due, at the promulgation of this sentence, except the just dues of the laundress; to be dishonorably discharged from the service of the United States and then to be confined at hard labor under charge of the guard at Alcatraz Island, Cal., or such other place of confinement as the Department Commander may order, for the period of ten years, wearing a ball weighing twelve pounds, attached to his leg by a chain five feet long.

The proceedings and findings in the foregoing case of Private Edgar Maynard, alias Joseph K. Dunlap, Company B, 4th Infantry [sic] was approved. The sentence is confirmed and will be duly executed.

Alcatraz Island, Cal. is designated as the place of confinement, to which the prisoner will be sent under proper guard.

The report of the court-martial does not include the testimony of Lawler, nor is there any report that Privates James Malone, Leopold Eith, James Henry, or J. Wilcox knew Maynard. Nevertheless, Lawler's assistance in the burglar's conviction and Maynard's harsh sentence angered many of the men at Fort Whipple. By 1876 Lawler, Malone, Eith, and other members of the 19th Infantry had been transferred to Fort Mojave. On January 10, 1876, a group of soldiers from Company K, 19th Infantry, gathered in the post trader's store at Fort Mojave and were "drinking deeply." Among them were Richard L. Lawler, James Malone, Leopold Eith, James Henry, and J. Wilcox. The soldiers became drunk and rowdy and overstayed their welcome, so they were ordered to leave the store. However, before they departed they purchased a supply of whiskey and continued their drinking outdoors, in the vicinity of the store, until the late hours. Lawler, a heavy drinker, imbibed to excess and finally became stupefied from the liquor. He was unsteady on his feet but managed to stumble around the building and find himself a place to lie down, and he tried to sleep so he could recover before returning to the fort. Lawler was unpopular among most of the men of the company because of his appearance as a witness against Maynard, but he was particularly detested by Malone because of the obnoxious manner in which Lawler had discharged his duties while a noncommissioned officer in Company K.

Malone, Eith, and the other soldiers found Lawler asleep and at Malone's urging immediately proceeded to put into execution a diabolical scheme. Stones and adobes were gathered and stacked and, when all the ammunition was in place, the disabled man was stoned to death, his head crushed in and his body horribly mutilated and mangled. Only a slight resistance was offered by the victim because he was in too drunk a state to rise from the ground as the attack began, and after the first few blows were struck he was thoroughly disabled. The murderers carried Lawler's dead body to the Colorado River, relying upon its swift current to carry away the corpse and all evidence of their crime. They were confident that if the body were not found near the store, they could not be implicated in his death and, if it was not found at all, it would be supposed Lawler had deserted. Malone and his companions returned to the post and rolled into their bunks, certain that they were free from discovery and arrest. However, Lawler's body was swept into a bayou or slough of the river where the current did not reach it, and there it remained trapped and floating. The quickly discovered body was immediately reported to authorities and recovered, and an inquest was ordered. The coroner's jury determined that a murder had been committed, and as a result of the finding an investigation began. The evidence soon pointed primarily to Malone and Eith, but it also indicated two others were involved. It was determined to be a federal civil matter as the scene of the crime was off the post. Malone, Eith, Henry, and Wilcox were arrested and indicted by the US grand jury, and their trials were set for the June 1877 term of the district circuit court. Henry turned state's evidence, testified against Malone and Eith, and was released in consideration of his cooperation. There was not enough evidence to implicate Wilcox, so he was released as well.

Malone and Eith had asked for and received separate trials. Malone was tried first and convicted of murder in the first degree on June 30, 1877. Judge C. A. Tweed sentenced the prisoner to hang. Eith was then tried and the jury found him guilty of first-degree murder on July 3, 1877, and the same sentence was then passed on Eith after the motion for a new trial and motion in arrest of judgment were overruled. Eith insisted he was innocent, but Judge Tweed said,

It is with the greatest feeling of pity and commiseration for you that I now discharge the painful duty of pronouncing against you the judgment of the law. The Court has no doubt of the correctness and propriety of the verdict rendered by the jury by which you were tried. It was apparent to the Court, upon the trial of your confederate Malone, that the proofs made by the prosecution in that case were conclusive of your guilt, and these proofs (were) made against you at your trial. It very rarely occurs that in a case where the proof is wholly circumstantial the guilt is so conclusively proved as in your case. Not one incident alone, but another and another and another pointed directly at, and connected you with the crime committed on that night of the 10th of January. The story of that night's crime was written in blood upon your own cast-off and concealed apparel, upon the spot where your victim was slain, and on the stones and sand over the long way where the body was dragged to the banks of the river, almost as distinctly and clearly as it was told by your confederate, Malone, the day after the deed was done.

The judge then pronounced the sentence, "It remains for me but to pronounce the judgment and sentence of the law, which is that you,

Leopold Eith, are guilty of murder, and that you be removed hence to the county jail or other place of confinement and there securely kept until the day hereafter be fixed for your execution and that on that day you will be taken to the place of execution and then and there be hanged by the neck until you are dead, and may you through sincere penitence and contrition obtain forgiveness and pardon for your great sin."

The cases were appealed and affirmed at the territorial level, and the US Supreme Court then affirmed the findings and sentences of the district court. The evidence in Eith's case was not as strong as in Malone's, so when applications for a commutation of their sentences to life imprisonment were submitted, Eith's commutation was granted and Malone's was denied. The killing of one soldier by another was a federal offense, so Eith was expected to be sent to a prison outside the Arizona Territory, most probably the House of Corrections at Detroit, Michigan, which was under contract with the US government, to serve out his term. However, on June 11, 1880, the grand jury committee for the 3rd Judicial District in Yavapai County consisting of H. A. Bigelow, W. Z. Wilson, and Philip Richardson reported:

The following report (to the judge) was adopted:

Col. C. P. Head, foreman of the Grand Jury—Sir: The committee appointed to examine into the case of the US Prisoners confined in the county jail report that we have visited the prisoners and find Leopold Eith . . . in confinement; and there is nothing special in the case of Eith, whose term of confinement will soon expire. . . .

On Friday, March 15, 1878, at 1:35 p.m., Malone arrived at the county jail from the Fort Whipple guardhouse, where he had been held since being sentenced to hang. He was transported by US Marshal Wiley W. Standifer, who was in charge of the execution, and the marshal was assisted by Deputy Marshals Joseph W. Evans and E. P. Raines. The condemned man was attended by Catholic priest Father Becker, his spiritual adviser, who was assisted by Reverend Alexander Gilmore and Reverend D. B. Wright. The door into the jail yard was thrown open to those holding tickets at 1:40 p.m., and sixty people rushed in and took their places near the gallows. The crowd was very orderly, "though many a pale face was seen among the gathering." The jail fence and the adjacent house tops "were covered with a swarm of figures, numbering nearly one hundred fifty, intent on catching every feature of the dreadful scene including the gallows on which Manuel Abiles had been hanged on August 6, 1875." Abiles had been the first man legally hanged in Yavapai County and only the second to be executed in the territory.

At 1:45 p.m. the prisoner stepped into the yard while tightly clutching his crucifix. Walking on his right was Marshal Standifer, while on his left was Father Becker. Deputy Marshal Evans and Reverends Gilmore and Wright brought up the rear of the procession. Malone walked firmly to the steps and ascended onto the platform of the scaffold without assistance, and he took his place on the trapdoor facing north. As soon as the prisoner was in place, Marshal Standifer read the death warrant signed by Judge Tweed and the judge's order to the marshal authorizing the execution. Malone requested that a confession written by him the previous night be read, and Reverend Wright, in a clear, perfectly audible voice, made public the last statement of the doomed man. It stated, in substance, that he was innocent of any participation in the crime and that he merely knew of its commission at the time by accident. His story had evolved over time and he now blamed Henry and Wilcox for the murder, emphasizing the irony that the two men who were guilty of Lawler's murder were now set free. He said he had family in the East, a mother and brother living at 123 East 11th Street, New York City, to whom it would be some consolation to know that he was guiltless of the heinous murder. He insisted that he made this statement knowing he was about to die and he rested his hopes for the hereafter on its truthfulness. While Reverend Wright spoke, Malone's wrists and ankles were bound with straps, and after the reverend concluded the reading of the confession, the black hood was pulled over the prisoner's head. However, Malone asked that it be removed so he could greet and shake hands with some of the soldiers from Fort Whipple whom he noticed were present among the witnesses. The hood was removed and Malone called to a sergeant and to several of the troopers he recognized, and they ascended the stairs and managed to shake hands with the prisoner. He bade them farewell in a hearty, offhanded way, as if he were only going on a short trip. He next shook hands with Deputy Marshal Evans and Marshal Standifer, and he asked the latter to be careful to adjust the noose properly and to "make a good job of it." He then asked for a drink and an alcoholic stimulant was provided.

Father Becker performed the last rites of the Catholic Church before the black hood was drawn over the prisoner's head for the second time. The noose of three-quarter-inch hemp was placed around Malone's neck, carefully positioned, and cinched tightly in place so it could not shift. At exactly 2:15 p.m. the trapdoor was sprung and the prisoner dropped five feet. A scarcely perceptible convulsive movement of Malone's chest and left arm followed, and then the body hung motionless. Doctor John Goodfellow was the physician in charge, and he reported that by 2:20 the pulse was barely perceptible. At 2:24, nine minutes after the trapdoor was sprung, Goodfellow pronounced Malone dead. The body was allowed to hang a total of twenty-one minutes, to ensure that he could not be revived, and then the remains were cut down and deposited in the cheap wooden coffin provided by Yavapai County. James Malone was buried in the Citizen's Burying Ground that evening, with a service conducted by the Catholic Church.

The hanging of James Malone

CHAPTER 2

"Good-bye, boys!"

Dennis W. Dilda was born on a farm near Rome, Georgia, in 1849. In his twenties he left home to avoid arrest after he stabbed a Negro to death for his money. He traveled to Texas, where he was soon charged with murdering a white man. Dilda fled and was pursued, captured, tried, and acquitted, but there appears to be no record of either the crime or his trial. After being freed in Texas, he met and married his wife, Georgia, and they soon followed her family from Texas to the Salt River Valley in the Arizona Territory. Over the next several years, Dilda got into several shooting scrapes in Phoenix, though no one was injured, but when his brother-in-law began to object to his sister's choice of a husband, the brother-in-law disappeared under suspicious circumstances. His body was never found and the family never heard from him again. Dilda was suspected of foul play, but there was no evidence so Dilda was not charged. In July 1885, Dilda moved his wife and their two children, two-year-old Fern and one-year-old John, to Yavapai County and began working for gardener W. J. O'Neill. After two months Dilda saw his chance to work for himself, and, using his knowledge of farming gained during his youth, he applied in September for a job with H. W. Williscraft.

Brothers H. W. and J. B. Williscraft had moved together to the Walnut Creek area of Yavapai County, forty miles west of Prescott. They had been successful working together in ranching and farming in Canada, but H. W. Williscraft was anxious to have his own farm, so he bought out his brother's interest. Williscraft quickly discovered that he could not handle the farm alone and began looking for someone to take over the farming business. It was at that time that Dennis W. Dilda appeared, claiming to be an experienced farmer. In September 1885 an arrangement was made for Dilda to do the farming as a tenant on the property, and he moved his family into the Williscraft house. Williscraft had reserved one room in the large house for himself. Inside the room he kept a locked trunk containing some valuables, and he secured the door to the room with a hasp and a heavy padlock. Williscraft moved off the property but left "General Grant" Jenkins, who had been an employee of the Williscraft brothers for more than twenty years, as the general caretaker for the property. Williscraft visited the farm in early December and found Jenkins gone, and he questioned Dilda. According to Dilda, Jenkins had become tired of the place and complained continuously, and one morning he had just packed up and left. Williscraft also found that the padlock had been pried off his reserved room, the trunk had been ransacked, and a gold watch and two pistols were missing. Dilda denied entering the room, perhaps hoping that Williscraft would conclude Jenkins had broken in before leaving.

Williscraft was not fooled by his tenant farmer, and he swore out a warrant with Yavapai County Sheriff William Mulvenon charging Dilda with theft. Responsibility for service of the warrant fell upon Deputy Sheriff John M. Murphy, a man well known throughout the area. Murphy had been born in Boston, Massachusetts, in 1846 and apprenticed as a ship's carpenter, but in 1874 he left his home and drifted south and then west. He arrived in Prescott in 1878 and served as a deputy under Sheriffs Joseph R. Walker, Jacob Henkle, and William Mulvenon during the next eight years, and he belonged to fraternal and civic organizations, including the Prescott Rifles. Murphy and Williscraft arrived at the ranch of Charley Behm midday on December 20, 1885, and, following lunch, Murphy declined any assistance from Behm or Williscraft. He called at the Dilda house several times during that Sunday afternoon but Dilda was absent each time, reportedly off on a hunting trip. Shortly after dark he went again, this time armed with Behm's needle gun. Murphy was met at the door by Dilda's wife, who again informed him that her husband had not yet returned home.

The moon was full and the sky clear so there was plenty of light to see by as Deputy Murphy walked toward a point from which he could watch the house and wait for Dilda's return. However, Dilda's wife had lied, and Dilda was lying in wait behind the fence that surrounded the yard. When the officer had taken a few steps outside the yard, he was fired upon. Murphy was shot through the back, the bullet passing through and coming out the upper part of his left breast. Although he had received a mortal wound, Murphy turned partly around and fired one shot from Behm's gun, then took several steps toward Dilda before falling to the ground and bleeding to death almost immediately. Dilda dragged the deputy's body into the yard and folded it in two so it would fit into a gunny sack, and then he and his wife dragged the body through the house to the back bedroom where a trapdoor led into a cellar. He dropped the body in, climbed in after the sack, and buried the body three feet deep beneath the dirt floor. The digging took nearly the entire night, interrupted only by a brief visit from Williscraft.

When Murphy did not return to the home of Behm, where the deputy had left his horse, Behm had become suspicious. The two shots he'd heard concerned him, so Behm sent Williscraft to check around the Dilda home, warning him to be careful. Dilda's wife called her husband from the cellar when, in the bright moonlight, she saw their landlord lurking about. Dilda then tried to lure Williscraft into killing range, but Williscraft was too cautious. Williscraft left and he did not return until the next morning, when he found evidence of the murder. Williscraft alerted Behm and his neighbors, but Dilda had left on foot earlier armed with his .30 caliber Remington rifle, Behm's needle gun, and Murphy's .44 caliber revolver and cartridge belt, along with some clothing, supplies, and valuables belonging to Deputy Murphy. Dilda's horse, which apparently had bolted when he shot Murphy, was found the following morning still saddled and grazing behind a shed.

Meanwhile, a party of men had gathered, and they continued to search the Williscraft farm. An Indian tracker noticed wheelbarrow tracks from the house to a garden a hundred feet behind the house; the wheelbarrow had a heavy load going but no load on its return. They searched the area and noted nothing out of the ordinary until one man pulled at a sunflower and found that it was only loosely planted. Digging on the spot they found Jenkins' body buried four feet deep in a sitting position. He had been dead two weeks, killed by a ball from a musket loader that had torn off the top of his head. Dilda, after his conviction, would confess that he killed the old man on December 12 while Jenkins was bending over the wash basin preparing for breakfast "because I was tired of having him around." It was rumored, but never proven, that Dilda may have heard that the old man had seven hundred dollars in gold that he always carried on his person and he had killed Jenkins for the money.

Sheriff Mulvenon summoned a posse and was on Dilda's trail for two days. They came upon the fugitive sleeping under a tree near Ash Fork, got the drop on him, arrested him without resistance, and lodged him in the county jail at Prescott. A grand jury was impaneled the following morning and an indictment returned on two counts of first-degree murder. A pleading was made, a three-hour trial was held on December 30, the prisoner was convicted, and his sentence was passed, all in just forty hours after the indictment. Dilda received the news of his impending hanging "with the utmost composure" and declined to provide a full confession up to the moment of his execution. His last comment on the subject was, "You know it would be natural for a man in my position, if he could tell anything that would benefit him, he would do so, but I have nothing to say." Chief Justice John C. Shields then set the date and time for the execution at 2:00 p.m. on Friday, February 5, 1886.

On the night before his execution, the prisoner asked to be baptized into the Catholic Church, and a priest was summoned for the next morning. Dilda's last night was restless, as he would doze only to awaken suddenly with a startled scream. He arose at 8:00 a.m. and sat in the jail corridor awaiting the moment he would be taken out, but he refused to see the priest when he arrived. At 8:30 a.m. the prisoner's hair was cut and he was shaved by a barber, as he would not be trusted with a razor, and then he bathed and put on a new suit of clothes provided by the sheriff. After 9:00, as he had requested, he was taken to the Chinese restaurant at the rear of the Palace Saloon and treated to a hearty meal of various delicacies, and he joked with the officers guarding him while taking a full hour to eat. Next the condemned man had his picture taken with his wife and children, and at 11:00 a.m. Sheriff Mulvenon read the death warrant to the prisoner in the corridor of the jail, with the press and a few other witnesses present. Dilda spent the remainder of the morning smoking his pipe and pacing back and forth until the time came to form the procession to the gallows.

Promptly at 11:30 a.m. on February 5, 1886, the condemned man was brought out of the jail, wrists bound in front, and placed in a waiting barouche. A large crowd of people had loitered around the jail all forenoon in hopes of getting a glimpse of the prisoner, and as Dilda came out he glanced around the crowd and yelled, "Good-bye, boys!" From the moment of bidding good-bye to the crowd around the old brick courthouse until he reached the scaffold, the prisoner did not speak a word. In the barouche was Sheriff Mulvenon, Sheriff Robert Stein of Mohave

Dennis and Georgia Dilda with children Fern (left) and John (right)

PHOTO COURTESY OF SHARLOT HALL MUSEUM LIBRARY AND ARCHIVES, PRESCOTT, AZ: PO-1025P

County, ex-sheriffs of Yavapai County Joseph R. Walker and Jacob Henkle, and Prescott's chief of police. The vehicle containing the prisoner was escorted from the courthouse to the scaffold by the Prescott Rifles and Prescott Grays. Following the barouche was a long line of rented hacks, buggies, carriages, buckboards, spring wagons, freight and ore wagons, and just about any type of wheeled vehicle that could join in the parade, as well as many spectators afoot. On arrival at the gallows the rifle companies were drawn up in a hollow square around the scaffold to keep the many spectators from crowding in.

Dilda, from the time he came in sight of the scaffold, never took his eyes from it. He ascended the steps of the scaffold as firm as any of the officers accompanying him. When asked if he had anything to say, he asked if Reverend Green was present but, upon being informed that he was not, said that he had nothing to say except for a request of Sheriff Mulvenon that his body be sent to his wife in Phoenix. Dilda was then directed to step onto the trapdoor, which he did, and he was asked, "Is there anything you want?" and he replied, "a drink."

The sheriff produced a whiskey bottle, and the prisoner drank deeply as George Burton busied himself pinioning the prisoner's knees and ankles. Dilda's arms and wrists were then strapped behind him by Deputies Michael Hickey and Burton. Hickey pulled the black hood over the prisoner's head and the noose was adjusted by Deputy James Tackett. The moment all was in readiness. Sheriff Mulvenon pulled the bar that released the trapdoor, and Dilda's body shot downward, just three minutes from the time he stepped onto the trapdoor, and two convulsive shudders of the body and a drawing up of his limbs twice were the only movements perceived. The execution was witnessed by nearly eight hundred men, but there were also a dozen females from the dance halls and prostitution cribs. The only commotion occurred when W. O. "Bucky" O'Neill, reporting for the *Hoof and Horn*, fainted as Dilda was dropped through the trapdoor.

Doctor Frank K. Ainsworth, the county physician, assisted by Fort Whipple's post surgeon Dr. C. C. Barrows, timed the pulsations of his heart, which fluctuated until the fourteenth minute, when there was only an irregular fluttering; and at the end of the fifteenth minute, Dilda was pronounced dead. The body was cut down and placed in a coffin. Upon removal of the black hood and noose, an examination showed that Dilda's neck had been broken in the fall, and the doctors insisted that his death had been instantaneous and painless. The body was given to undertaker Randall and driven to the cemetery, in spite of the deceased's request to be sent to his wife in Phoenix, and within half an hour from the time the noose was adjusted around his neck Dilda was safely stowed away in his grave, without ceremony or service. There had been a rumor that Mrs. Dilda had vowed to avenge her husband's death if he was hanged, but the rumor proved false and she had not even requisitioned her husband's body to be sent to Phoenix.

CHAPTER 3

Betrayal of a Benefactor

Frederick Hopt, alias Fred Welcome, was born near the Dutch villages of Pennsylvania in 1858. He visited Germany with his parents in 1863 and the following year returned to America, where his family settled in Indiana. Two years later the family moved to Minnesota, and when Hopt reached the age of majority, he left home and moved to Illinois. There he learned the harness trade, returned to Minnesota for a brief period, then traveled to California, started east to Nevada, and finally settled in Utah. Hopt was arrested on July 1, 1879, for stealing a horse. Sheriff John W. Turner of Utah County held him for trial, but when the complaining witness moved to Montana, Turner petitioned for Hopt's release. This was granted in October and Hopt, who was without funds, was hired by the sheriff to do light work and odd jobs. In mid-December Hopt said he wanted to go to Park City, so Turner gave him money, blankets, and other necessities and bid him farewell. However, Hopt did not leave town but instead used the money given him by the sheriff to go on a drunken spree, and he was arrested the following day and fined ten dollars. Hopt, upon his release, left for Park City that evening after making threats against Sheriff Turner and his family.

John F. Turner, the sheriff's twenty-four-year-old son, had been teaming in various mining camps for three seasons and had been successful in that line of work. He had two good wagons, two span of fine

Hopt's victim, John F. Turner
AUTHOR COLLECTION

horses, a general camping outfit, and a ton and a half of chopped barley. Some of the grain was in unmarked sacks while some was in sacks imprinted JOHN F. TURNER, PROVO. On June 28, 1880, he left Provo for Park City to look for work as a teamster. On July 1 he met Hopt who, being familiar with the area, escorted young Turner through the various camps surrounding the town. During the day Hopt abruptly disappeared, but he returned in the evening and drove one of the teams to Turner's camp and stayed with Turner the next two days. On July 3 Hopt was seen driving one of Turner's teams, and later that day he talked with W. H. Hook of Gunnison, Colorado. Hopt told Hook that he was going to Wyoming and had two teams to sell, and he asked Hook to accompany him and drive one team and Hook agreed. During the early evening hours, Hopt was seen at Turner's camp, and at nine o'clock he and Turner met Hook and Jack Emerson in Creek & Dodge's Saloon. Hopt went outside, beckoning Emerson to follow, and they left Turner with Hook, who kept the young man occupied with conversation for five minutes. When Turner left the saloon, he could not find Hopt, so he returned to his camp alone.

After talking with Emerson, Hopt went to the local druggist and tried to buy strychnine "to kill the rats which are eating my grain at camp," but the druggist would not sell him the poison. Hopt was next seen after ten o'clock with blood staining his shirt front. When questioned about the blood, he said he had a fight "with a s__ of a b___ and struck him and struck him hard." Hopt then went back and forth between the dance hall and the saloon, drinking and dancing the rest of the night. He spent Independence Day at the race track, and he had arrived there riding one of Turner's horses. After noon he asked Pat Egan to drive one of his two teams to Montana, but Egan listened to Hopt's proposal, examined the teams, and decided not to go. Early Tuesday morning, July 6, Hopt and Emerson drove the two outfits eastward with Turner's body covered up in the bed of the first wagon, which was open. Emerson pulled up the second covered wagon at Snyder's barn to collect his belongings, and Hopt, obviously anxious, called to him to hurry along. Another young man, who also slept in Snyder's barn, asked Emerson where they were going, and Emerson replied they were going to Payne's Canyon. Four miles east of Park City, Hopt and Emerson, now both on the front wagon, were seen by Sheriff Allison of Summit County, who was returning to town by stagecoach, and he saw Hook driving the second wagon. The three men were next seen when they stopped at Wanship, a dozen miles from Park City, and Hopt sold some of the grain there. The grain was in the rear wagon, where Emerson, now drunk, was lying down upon the sacks, and Hopt was careful to sell only the sacks that had no imprint on them. The men and teams were next seen passing through Coalville, twenty-four miles from Park City, and five miles farther from there they reached the mouth of Echo Canyon. They were seen turning their wagons into the canyon, and they proceeded nine miles before they made camp. The next day, July 7, they continued on.

At Evanston, Wyoming, Hopt sold the grain with Turner's imprint on the sacks, and at Piedmont he sold one span of horses and a wagon to W. H. Moss for two hundred dollars, signing the bill of sale and having Emerson witness the transaction. At Green River he sold the second team and wagon to Mr. Hall for $225. Money weighing heavily in his pockets, Hopt went to Berry's Saloon in Green Valley, argued with the saloon's owner, and drew his pistol. He was immediately subdued by the patrons and disarmed, and he said, "I wouldn't kill anybody, I never did." Then he paused for a moment and said, "Yes I did. I killed a young man in cold blood, and I killed him with an axe." He was not taken seriously, and two days later Hopt parted company with Emerson and Hook and left town by train with new companion George Roach.

On July 11 a boy by the last name of Phillips was fishing with his father when he found the body of young Turner lying on the side of a mountain behind a large rock nine miles inside Echo Canyon. The corpse was rolled up in a tent and covered with large rocks, some weighing from ninety to one hundred pounds, and lucerne leaves and brush were piled on top. When the tent was unrolled, it was discovered that the murderer had tried to cremate the body but apparently could not get it to burn. Turner was clothed in a shirt, undershirt, drawers, and pantaloons, with one sock turned down as if he was struck dead while removing it. The left side of the dead man's head was crushed in from a blow from the blunt edge of an axe, and the area under the jaw was broken by a glancing blow from the same kind of weapon. About the time the body was found in Echo Canyon, Hopt and Roach arrived in Rawlins, Wyoming, and Hopt went on a drunken spree and began courting an abandoned woman; after several days of these shenanigans, Roach became uneasy and departed. On July 14 Hopt bought a train ticket to Laramie but, once aboard, paid his fare through to Cheyenne, where he took a room at Dwyer's Hotel. Over the next ten days, Hopt spent lavishly on hired livery teams and sporting women until, by July 23, he had spent nearly every stolen dollar and was indebted for board and livery fees.

On July 19 Sheriff Turner received a telegram asking if Hopt's title was valid for the team he had sold to Moss at Piedmont. The sheriff left immediately to investigate, arrived in Park City on July 20, and then learned of the inquest to be conducted on a body found

Frederick Hopt
SAN FRANCISCO CHRONICLE: AUGUST 12, 1887

in Echo Canyon. He changed his destination to Coalville and from there went with Sheriff Allison to Echo. After identifying his son's body, Turner made arrangements to have the remains shipped to Salt Lake City. The two sheriffs, now in pursuit of Hopt, took the train to Piedmont and found the covered wagon and team stolen from Turner's son. At Green River they found the open wagon, which had lucerne leaves and clotted blood in the bed, along with the murder weapon, the axe. They continued on to Rawlins and searched the entire day of July 22 but did not find Hopt, so the next day they took the train east to Cheyenne. Along the way they stopped at Laramie, where Turner delayed long enough to telegraph two detective agencies, one in Omaha and the other in Kansas City, to be on the lookout for Hopt. Upon arriving in Cheyenne Turner made several inquiries without success, but when he stepped onto the depot's platform he saw Hopt standing fifty yards away. Hopt was immediately arrested, but Turner could not control his anger and attacked Hopt, screaming, "You murdered my son!" while strangling the prisoner. The murderer was saved by two lawmen who pulled Turner away and restrained him, and then Hopt said, as if it was a foregone conclusion, "I will hang for this when I get back to Utah." One of the detectives, who had not been informed of the situation, asked Hopt what he had done to cause Turner to attack him so violently, and the prisoner made the first in a series of confessions. Hopt was released to Turner, who had regained his composure, and they began the return trip to Salt Lake City. When the train reached Rawlins at midnight, a large party of citizens asked Turner to hand over the prisoner so they could lynch him. However, the sheriff refused and eventually convinced them to let the law take its course. At Green River Mr. Hall and twenty citizens threatened to take the prisoner from the sheriff and hang him from the railroad bridge, but Turner's pleas again prevailed. At Echo more than twenty citizens demanded the life of Hopt, but Turner once again talked the mob out of a lynching. Turner and his prisoner finally arrived at Salt Lake City, and Hopt was lodged in jail to await the action of the grand jury.

On December 14, 1880, Fred Hopt and Jack Emerson, whose real name was John McCormick, were indicted for first-degree murder. Emerson turned state's evidence to avoid the death penalty and was tried on October 20, 1881. He was sentenced to life in prison in consideration of his testimony against Hopt, and he served a little more than five years before he was pardoned. Hopt was tried on February 16, 1881, convicted, and sentenced to be shot; but the decision and sentence were reversed by the US Supreme Court. The second trial began on March 2, 1883, and Hopt was again convicted, but this time he was sentenced to hang. The conviction was again reversed by the US Supreme Court, so Hopt's third trial began on April 29, 1884, and the defendant was again convicted and this time sentenced to be shot. The case was appealed to the territorial and then again to the US Supreme Court. The execution had not been stayed and the territorial court now lacked jurisdiction, so Governor Eli H. Murray authorized a respite until the case could be heard, and in April 1886 the US Supreme Court once again reversed the conviction on a technicality. The fourth trial of Fred Hopt began on September 21, 1886, and the defendant was once again convicted; this time Hopt was sentenced to be shot on November 24. The conviction and sentence were appealed, which further delayed the execution, but finally the conviction was affirmed on March 7, 1887, and on June 24 the court rescheduled Hopt's execution for August 11, 1887. During Hopt's long imprisonment he studied law and had become as familiar with the legal points of his case as his counsel, so he was aware that all that remained to save him was a plea for clemency. Several men and numerous women pled for a reprieve and circulated petitions for a commutation of sentence on the grounds that "the poor, persecuted murderer had suffered enough." However, on August 1 Governor Caleb W. West informed Hopt's counsel that he would not interfere.

Hopt distributed his few personal belongings three days prior to his execution. On August 10 Marshal Frank H. Dyer talked with Hopt regarding the manner of the execution and the disposition of his remains, and Hopt made a request to the penitentiary physician in writing that his body not be dissected. He then asked that his body be buried near the prison until his friends could move it to a more sacred place. A reporter was admitted and Hopt was, at first, reluctant to talk. Finally he explained all the details that proved him innocent, and then he complained that in his second and subsequent trials his defense witnesses could not be found. The prison warden interrupted the interview to ask if the prisoner objected to photographs of the execution, and he refused to sanction it. After Hopt refused to have the execution photographed, he also refused to speak further with the reporter.

The prisoner passed a sleepless final night, but at seven o'clock he arose and ate a hearty breakfast. A Catholic priest, Father Kelly of All Hallows College, was with Hopt the entire morning of August 11, providing spiritual consolation and administering the sacrament. The execution was delayed thirty minutes at Hopt's request so he could eat a good dinner. At 12:15 p.m. the other prisoners were locked in their bunkhouses, in which the north windows were sealed to prevent them from watching the event, while the prison physician gave Hopt final instructions on how he was to sit in the chair. Meanwhile the five members of the firing squad had been brought to the penitentiary and placed in the warden's apartment. Each member was covered head to ankle in black cambric, and at 12:20 p.m. they were sent to the twelve-foot-by-fourteen-foot tent pitched in the northeast corner of the prison quadrangle. Two deputies had delivered five .45-.70 Winchester rifles to the tent earlier, and a board bench along the north wall of the tent accommodated the executioners, as each sat in front of one of five three-inch square holes cut in the north side of the canvas. Thirty feet away, fifteen feet south of the north wall, a blanket was spread on the ground and a common chair positioned in the center. At 12:30 p.m. the procession filed out of the prison toward the place of execution, with Marshal Dyer escorting Hopt in front. The condemned man was dressed in a black diagonal suit, white shirt and tie, oxford shoes, and Derby hat, and he smoked a cigar as they marched. Hopt was followed by his priest, the prison physician, and another doctor who was assisting him; next came his friend Royal B. Young, who had stayed with Hopt to the last; then came three deputies marching in step with the procession; and last were two more deputy sheriffs who remained in the background. Hopt threw his cigar down as he took his place in the chair. When asked if he wished to make a statement, he arose, removed his hat, and said, "Gentlemen, I have come to meet my fate. Had justice been done me at my first trial, I would not be here today for this purpose. I have no ill-will toward any man living, and am prepared and ready to meet my God."

Hopt sat down, put on his hat, and then declined to be blindfolded. The prison physician carefully pinned a one-and-one-half-inch paper circle over the prisoner's heart, and the condemned man shook hands with each official standing by his chair. Hopt then placed his hands on his legs, took a deep breath, relaxed, and waited patiently. The officials and Young stepped back some distance while Marshal Dyer took his place at the corner of the firing-squad tent. The marshal asked, "Are you ready, gentlemen?" and they replied that they were, so the marshal closed the tent flaps as he warned, "Be very careful, now." He then announced, "Make ready!" followed quickly by "Aim!" and then at 12:40 p.m. he ordered "Fire!" and five rifles discharged as one. The condemned man rolled back his eyes, dropped his underlip, and fell over backward, killed instantly. The four bullets (one rifle was loaded with a blank) entered in a line eight inches long and exited in a line four inches long, with the top two piercing Hopt's heart and each of the lead balls breaking a rib entering and exiting. Father Kelly quickly stepped forward and administered extreme unction to the dead man's lips.

The undertaker quickly brought forward the coffin, which had been purchased by Marshal Dyer. It was made of redwood with silver trim, highly polished and inscribed Rest in Peace. Hopt's remains were deposited within, and the coffin was carried by four deputies and two guards to the prison vestibule, where it lay on display for a brief period. The body was then transported into the city, where a crowd of more than two thousand people viewed the murderer's remains at Skewes' Undertaking Parlor on Third South Street. The following day Hopt was buried in the Catholic cemetery following a brief service by Father Kelly.

CHAPTER 4

"The shadow of death hovering o'er me."

During the latter part of July 1888, twenty-eight-year-old George Duncan Bryson and forty-five-year-old Annie Lundstrom arrived in Helena and took rooms with Sarah Bennett at 310 Bridge Street. Bryson introduced Lundstrom to everyone as his wife and she went by the name Bryson, but she did not behave as a wife would be expected to behave toward her husband regarding money. While at Mrs. Bennett's boardinghouse, the couple quarreled frequently, and on more than one occasion Lundstrom told her landlady that she feared for her life. The quarrels were always about money, with Bryson demanding more money while Lundstrom insisted on providing funds in small amounts. Lundstrom told Mrs. Bennett that she thought Bryson would leave her if he got hold of all her money, and she said she feared that he might even kill her for it. She told her landlady she had converted her money and distributed it among several drafts that she had sewn into different dresses and other clothing so that, if Bryson found some of the drafts, he would not find all of her wealth. Lundstrom wore a large gold chain with a handsome distinctive watch, and she wore a switch, a tuft of hair, to cover the bald spot on the crown of her scalp. However, though she feared that Bryson would harm her or rob her, she was quite infatuated with the younger man and feared even more that he would leave her. The couple stayed with Mrs. Bennett two weeks, and on August 4 Bryson and Lundstrom moved to the boardinghouse of

Mrs. Trunk at 516 Eighth Avenue, where Lundstrom paid a month's rent in advance. Mrs. Trunk had two other boarders, Mrs. Mixture and Mrs. Hardwick, and the residents all became acquainted with the couple—and soon became familiar with their incessant quarreling. Lundstrom developed a close relationship with Mrs. Mixture and repeated to her the fear that Bryson would take all her money and then leave her, or that he might kill her. On August 21, when Bryson returned home at 2:00 p.m. and the couple left to have dinner, all the ladies were present and particularly noticed Lundstrom's clothing when she left. Two hours later Bryson returned alone and went to his room, but he soon left and went uptown. He returned at a late hour and spent the rest of the night pacing in his room. In the morning Mrs. Trunk learned that Bryson had packed their trunks during the night and at seven o'clock he left to get expressman Joe Ryan. He explained that his wife, Lundstrom, had gone on to Butte and he would be joining her later, and then he moved out.

Mrs. Mixture was immediately suspicious, as that morning Lundstrom had asked her to change a ten-dollar bill and then asked her to keep five dollars until she returned from dinner, so Mrs. Mixture told Mrs. Trunk of that development. Mrs. Trunk then disclosed that the rent was paid for two more weeks but there had been no demand for a rebate when Bryson moved out early. Still, Mrs. Mixture waited three weeks, but finally she could not restrain her fears any longer and reported the matter to the police. She had pictures of Bryson and Lundstrom, given to her by the latter, and she gave them to the officers. A reporter for the Helena *Independent* newspaper then made the public aware of Lundstrom's absence and the possibility of foul play.

A search was made throughout Helena for Bryson, but he could not be found. There was no clue to Lundstrom's whereabouts, though it was confirmed she had never arrived in Butte. However, one day a

George Bryson
HELENA INDEPENDENT: AUGUST 10, 1889

Victim Annie Lundstrom
HELENA INDEPENDENT: AUGUST 10, 1889

woman appeared at the post office and asked for Bryson's mail, and she deposited a watch at the post office for safekeeping. When she reappeared two days later, lawmen were waiting and surreptitiously followed her to a small hotel near the Northern Pacific Railroad depot, which was kept by a woman named Mrs. Porter. There they found that Bryson was living with Flora Thompson, the woman they had shadowed. Bryson was arrested on suspicion of foul play, and he explained that Lundstrom had gone on to Seattle, contradicting his first story that she had gone to Butte. He refused to say where their luggage was located. The lawmen backtracked and learned that after the fugitive left Mrs. Trunk's boardinghouse, he went to the Lenoir House, where he registered as J. D. Lundstrom and had his luggage with him. The following day he moved to the hotel where he was captured. He registered under the alias Mr. Barnes from Seattle, but he had little luggage. A preliminary examination was conducted and Bryson was held to answer to the grand jury based entirely upon circumstantial evidence, as the body of Lundstrom had not been found.

A reward of three hundred dollars was then offered by the mayor for the recovery of the body, which was not found until October 1 when a blacksmith named Dixon stumbled upon the remains of a woman in the bottom of a prospect hole northeast of the city. Though in a terrible state of decomposition, the remains were identified by the clothing Lundstrom was last seen wearing on August 21, and the distinctive watch left at the post office was identified as Lundstrom's. At the inquest the jury found that Lundstrom had died at the hands of Bryson, and the grand jury returned a true bill (indictment) against the prisoner charging him with one count of murder. The prisoner was arraigned and then the judge granted a change of venue to Jefferson County, where the trial commenced at Boulder in early March 1889. Bryson's trial concluded on March 16 with the jury, after sixteen hours of deliberation, returning a verdict of guilty of first-degree murder. The motion for a new trial was denied and on appeal the territorial supreme court affirmed the decision of the lower court. Bryson's appeal and the petition for a commutation of sentence submitted to Governor Benjamin F. White were denied, and he was re-sentenced to hang on August 9, 1889. On the day before his execution, Bryson wrote out his final statement to be read on the scaffold, and it included a comprehensive presentation of the evidence offered by the prosecution and his defense:

Boulder, Mont. Aug. 9—To the citizens of Montana and the world: See the shadow of death hovering o'er me; see the instrument of death to be dealt out to a stranger in your land. Over your hills I came with a friend less than a year ago; that friend has, to all accounts, gone to her last resting place. Are you positive? No, you are not. Is it the friend that I left at the Montana Central depot? Can you answer yes? You cannot. True it was her clothes, by the marks, but whose body was in those clothes? Was it identified? Never. Why was I not called on to identify? Let us say that it was Annie Lundstrom and pass on to my guilt.

Have you any evidence to conclusively prove that the poor young man standing before you to-day committed the crime? You have none whatever. True, you have circumstances and suppositions that speak volumes, but what do they prove? Can you hang a man on such evidence? Evidently you can. Without remorse you take the evidence as gospel of people who have no regard for the truth whatever. Paid hirelings of the law take the evidence of Mrs. Hardwick and Mixture, two of the main witnesses of the prosecution. Do you believe Them? Which of these stories do you believe, her first at the preliminary examination of the one in the district court of this city, or do you believe any or any part of her evidence? Her first was that the defendant in this case came home about 9:30 o'clock on the evening Mrs. Lundstrom disappeared, lit a lamp and commenced taking down the things from the wall and packing them in the trunks, also that he made considerable noise, and she doubted very much whether I slept any all night; and as to the loud talking she heard, she could not really call it a quarrel. What does story No. 2 say? That the defendant came home about 10 o'clock, sneaked in, made no noise whatsoever, got up at an unusual hour in the morning. When asked as to the house talk, she stated with vehemence in her speech and look that was concentrated indignation. Can any sane man believe such testimony and say you are guilty? She also identifies every prominent article in a stranger's trunk and says they were the woman's who disappeared. Mrs. Mixture does likewise. That white dress she made no one could make it. No one else wears white dresses. Oh, no! No one else has a sewing machine that sews just like her's [sic]. Where is the $5 bill Mrs. Lundstrom

31

left with her? Why was it not produced? Because she never left it with her. She did not have $5 to leave with her. Did I not have to give her money to buy a ticket to go to Butte? Now let me pass on to the evidence of detective Nels P. Walters. He says he found those articles in the prospect hole on the morning of March 4, along with other witnesses. How is it they were found immediately after I left Helena for this city? Why does he go up there with three or four men to do detective work? Because he put them there himself; secured his hirelings to substantiate his story and make an impression. How easy to take a ring and scratch the initials A. L. on it. How easy to take the hairpins and put them in the hole. How easy to take that handkerchief and put it there. How miraculously easy to take that pocketbook at the time the body was found and slip it in his pocket. You will agree with me gentlemen that, had those things been in that hole October 1st, 1888, they would have been found. You have a sample of his testimony when he swore that I said I bought the ticket for Mrs. Lundstrom at the depot along with Anthony Kuntz. Did we not have to put their own attorney on the stand and contradict them to establish the truth? I have never been to the prospect hole in question but I have common sense enough to know that Detective Walters committed perjury and the good people pay such a scoundrel $1,500 a year. Did the defense not prove to you without question this woman was seen in company with another man below the depot and again with a man of the same appearance going in the direction of the hole on the evening she disappeared. Did she not by the evidence of Mr. Chandler, have clandestine and probably criminal meetings with a man described specifically as above? Certainly she did. Did she ever inform her friend, myself, of it? No, she did not. Who is this man? Is he the one who killed Annie Lundstrom or not? It seems to most any level headed man that he knows something about her death. Take the hackman covered with

blood from head to foot. Why does he leave town on the very eve-
ning she disappeared and has not been seen since. Were these two
men in collusion with each other? Did they make the tracks leading
to the hole where the body was found. There must have been two
men in order to tie the woman's (wrists) the way they were tied
when found and secreted her in that hole. Who was the man or men
who has, by the evidence of Mr. Wright, had when the defendant in
this case was in jail in Helena, taken the pole out of that hole,
knocked the steps off and thrown it fully one hundred feet from the
hole, returned on the night previous to the body being found and
placed the pole back in the former position? I should judge to allay
suspicion. Does that man know who put that body there or not?
Most undoubtedly he does. How did Mr. Duncan Dixon find that
"Injun," as he termed it? Can you tell me in such metre in two hours
after the reward was offered he finds what the whole town of Hel-
ena was baffled to find in three and almost four weeks? Oh, my
friends, standing here as I do on the brink of the grave 'tis mon-
strous to behold, innocent as I am. Death is nothing, a mere whiff,
compared with the brand of shame which falls upon my child, my
offspring, her whom I love, next to God, better than all else in this
world; her image is engraved on my heart, never to be effaced only
when it ceases to be, and then to carry it with me to heaven and
paradise. Is it not safe to say that I have been convicted on public
sentiment? Do you call this a competent juror when he says he has
formed the opinion and that opinion is adverse to the prisoner in
the dock? Your statutes say nay. I had four just such jurors as that.
Had they been true and honest men they would have asked the
court to excuse them. One juror, when balloting as to the cause of
death, signed, "known" (meaning the cause of death). Was there any
evidence of death introduced to show the most gullible the cause of
death? None whatever. Gentlemen, you have found your verdict on

these principles. A woman was killed. Somebody had to suffer to satisfy the law. You picked a stranger upon your streets and said we have not enough evidence to convict him but hang he must. In conclusion I must state that the territory of Montana in hanging George Duncan Bryson commits a judicial murder, breaks the heart of the most noble father and mother in the world, and dishonors the most honorable name in Canadian history. Some day God will clear up this mystery. He will, no doubt reveal the guilty ones, and they will be justly punished. How, gentlemen of the jury, will you feel when I am vindicated in this statement and my name shall be set forth as another victim of circumstantial evidence? Will this nation continue to convict men on the same principle, or will they hesitate? Time will tell. Let me say a few words as to the press of Helena, the Independent *especially. I have yet to see a more bigoted, partisan newspaper. It stopped at nothing, even defaming my father and belittling him in the eyes of the public. The very first editorial introduced myself as a thief, burglar, highway robber, and to cap all a murderer. It printed the article on the uncorroborated testimony of one Frank Griswold Ward, now a discharged employee of the Union Pacific Tea company, Minneapolis. How honest in principle must have been that respected and renowned man, editor* Independent. *What an example of morality and uprightness the former at the time he wrote to the authorities at Helena was selling coffee at 25 cents a pound and putting 12½ cents of the money received into his own pocket. Oh, people, you stand around me today some out of morbid curiosity, others out of sympathy, and others to do their sworn duty. Take a little advice, strangers, Avoid bad company. It has swayed nations; yes, it has ruined some. It has ruined me, and bowed my head in shame. The only consolation I have that in my way consoles me is the knowledge that in the future my relatives, though smarting from the injustice done me, will be grasped by the hand, and greeted with the exclamation—your brother was innocent, and some day his honor will be vindicated. But the grandest consolation of all is that God has offered me his love, and will so guide me in this dreaded hour through that narrow path to his palatial abode, saved through the Lord, Jesus Christ, my Savior and Redeemer.*

Truthfully yours,
George Duncan Bryson

The prisoner's father stayed with him while he received visitors until 10:00 p.m. and left when the jail closed. After all the visitors were gone, Bryson talked with his guards and County Sheriff Dudley Halford, who agreed to sit with him until midnight as he awaited a message from Governor White. A fellow prisoner sang comic songs, and other inmates joined in. When the message regarding Bryson's commutation had not arrived by 1:00 a.m., the condemned man retired and slept soundly for five hours. When he awoke, he dressed in the light suit he had worn throughout his trial and then ate a hearty breakfast. Bryson's father returned to spend those last few hours with his son. At 9:00 a.m. the message finally arrived, but the governor said he could find no grounds for interference. As soon as it was certain the execution would proceed, Reverend Guiler conducted a religious service for Bryson, and afterward several ladies visited. After the ladies left the prisoner had a talk with his father, which was conducted in French so they could exclude others from understanding what they said. On August 6 Bryson had sent a telegram to his six-year-old daughter, Maude Chase Bryson, who lived with her mother in Howick, Ontario, Canada, pleading with her to come visit him. It was clearly too late for her to make the trip, and the telegram may have been a ploy to gain sympathy and encourage Governor White to grant a respite until she could arrive. When it became clear his daughter would not arrive in time, Bryson wrote her a long letter giving her advice on how to live her life and proclaiming his innocence. He gave it to his father to deliver, and the full text of the letter was published in the Prescott, Arizona Territory's *Miner* newspaper on August 9. When this was done he sent for Presbyterian Reverend I. A. Wickes, who joined Reverend Guiler and captain of Helena's Salvation Army post Leonard Bom, who had come to conduct prayers and songs. At 10:00 a.m. Bryson said his farewells to his father, shook hands with all his guards and the reporters, and then had a long confidential talk with Bom.

Sheriff Halford read the death warrant in the presence of local educator Professor Brown, Louis de Lestry, and Deputy Jerry Ellis, and the procession formed at 10:30 a.m. Bryson was conducted to the gallows, the same on which John P. Hart was hanged on February 10, 1888. The prisoner read his carefully prepared statement while the straps were being applied to his arms and legs. As soon as Bryson finished his harangue, he turned to Sheriff Halford and said, "Gentlemen, do your duty!" The noose was adjusted and then Bryson said his final words, "May God have mercy on my soul!" The hood was pulled over his head, and at 10:52 a.m. the axe fell, cutting the restraining rope. The gallows was a twitch-up design, and as the heavy counterpoise weight fell, it jerked Bryson into the air and his neck was broken in two places. There followed several convulsive movements before the body hung limp and motionless in seven minutes. Doctors Fletcher, Leighton, and Brooks were in attendance, and in nine and one half minutes they pronounced Bryson dead. Twelve minutes after the weight fell, Bryson's remains were cut down and placed in a plain wooden coffin. He was buried in the Boulder cemetery, at county expense, at 4:00 p.m.

CHAPTER 5

The Carlisle Kid

Nah-diez-az, a Pinal Indian, was born in 1865 along the Verde River in the Arizona Territory. In 1875, when Nah-diez-az was but ten years old, his tribe—along with the Yavapai tribe—was marched southward nearly two hundred miles during the winter months, including through a blinding blizzard. They were forced to settle on the San Carlos Indian Reservation among several other tribes, some of whom had been their enemies for centuries. The reservation, sometimes called "Hell's Forty Acres," had been established in 1871 for the Chiricahua tribe, and it was a place where summer temperatures could reach 120 degrees and winter temperatures could drop below freezing. The semi-arid land was nearly barren in most places but swampy in others, and malaria and many other diseases sometimes became epidemic. It was a terrible place for the Pinal tribe, which had lived in a rich, fertile mountainous region where the climate was cool and the air clean, and where there were large forests and ample water and game. Each Pinal family was allotted a plot of land to cultivate, and they tried to make the best of a terrible situation.

On November 1, 1879, the Carlisle School, the first nonreservation Indian school, opened its doors at the converted Carlisle army barracks in central Pennsylvania. Many of the students came north from the Apache tribes banished to Florida, but others came east from the San Carlos Indian Reservation near Tucson. Among the latter was fourteen-year-old Nah-diez-az, an only child who had farmed a small plot of reservation land with his mother and father. Some of the students did not do well in this new environment where school superintendent Lieutenant Richard Henry Pratt's philosophy was "kill the Indian in him, and save the man." In practice this turned many students inward and they became hostile, but Nah-diez-az appreciated the opportunity to learn and improve his prospects for adjusting and prospering in the white man's world. Those who accepted the learning process were described by historian James L. Haley as "white men in a red skin." Nah-diez-az became a well-regarded, or model, student at the school, and he did so well that he earned the sobriquet "the Carlisle Kid." He seemed the poster child for the school's motto: "To civilize the Indian, get him into civilization. To keep him civilized, let him stay."

The mother of Nah-diez-az died while he was away at school, so when his father took ill he was allowed to return and care for him. To survive, he had to again farm their plot of land, so as soon as he arrived he began to prepare their plot for planting. On March 10, 1887, Frank Porter, the Indian Agency's farm supervisor, went to the wickiup of twenty-two-year-old Nah-diez-az to inform him that he and his father were going to be moved to another plot, one far inferior to the plot upon which his family had lived for the past dozen years. Porter explained that the army had made plans to build a road through the reservation and it would pass over his plot of land. Nah-diez-az argued against the move and when the discussion became heated Porter, fearing violence, fled to the agency and strapped on his six-shooter. He went to the post and asked Captain Francis E. Pierce, 6th Cavalry, for assistance. The captain, who was the regimental quartermaster and acting Indian agent, assigned Lieutenant Seward Mott to accompany Porter on his return to the wickiup.

Twenty-five-year-old Mott was new to the army and new to the Arizona Territory, and not too familiar with the Indians on the reservation. He had graduated from the military academy in 1886 and had only arrived at San Carlos in July of that year, less than nine months earlier. Mott also wore his sidearm but he had no fear of a shooting affair as the Indians at San Carlos were not allowed to possess firearms, except for members of the agency's Indian police force. Mott and Porter rode together to the wickiup, but when Nah-diez-az saw two white men coming armed with pistols, to evict him or worse, he rushed into his wickiup and dug out the old Army colt his father had hidden years before and lovingly cared for regularly. The two men had dismounted while Nah-diez-az was about this business of digging up the pistol, so when the Indian emerged from the wickiup he immediately took aim at Porter and, without warning or hesitation, fired one shot. The boy was not familiar with pistols and probably had never fired one before, and his shot missed Porter but hit Mott, critically wounding the lieutenant. Mott collapsed and Porter, fearing for his life, mounted and rushed to the police-scout headquarters and reported the shooting. Al Seiber detailed agency policemen Mickey Free and Haskay-bay-nay-natyl, known as "Sergeant Kid," to bring in Nah-diez-az. The two Indian policemen rode to the wickiup and were surprised when Nah-diez-az came out with one hand raised and the other holding the pistol by the barrel, rather loosely. They arrested Nah-diez-az and took the unconscious lieutenant and their prisoner back to the post. Doctor T. B. Davis, post physician, gave the lieutenant all the care he could, but his wound was too severe and Mott died the following day without regaining consciousness. His body was returned to his hometown at Rockville, New York, and buried in the city cemetery.

Nah-diez-az was taken before Federal Judge W. W. Porter (no relation to Frank Porter) at the May term of the US Circuit Court. The defendant explained all the details that led to the shooting and pled guilty, but he asked for mercy from the court. The judge took the guilty plea, the explanation, and the plea for mercy into consideration and reduced the sentence from death to life imprisonment at the territorial prison near Yuma. Nah-diez-az was delivered to the territorial prison without incident, and he was at the prison during some of the hottest months of the year, when temperatures could reach 120 degrees. In the fall he was transferred to the Illinois Penitentiary which, along with a penitentiary at Columbus, Ohio, was under contract to the federal government, and he was expected to serve out the remainder of his life term. Other Indians, convicted of lesser crimes at about the same time, had been sent to the prison in Ohio and the Indian Rights Association became concerned with the suffering of the Indian prisoners in the Ohio Penitentiary, so they filed a case on behalf of those prisoners. When the US Supreme Court issued a writ of habeas corpus it was mistakenly interpreted as a pardon, so the ten Indians at the Ohio Penitentiary and Nah-diez-az at the Menard, Illinois, penitentiary were released. They returned to the San Carlos reservation, arriving at Willcox, Arizona Territory, in the custody of Lieutenant B. C. Lockwood of the 22nd Infantry at Columbus, Ohio, on May 24, 1889. They were released and all returned to the reservation the following day.

The citizens of Arizona were outraged by the release of eleven guilty, sentenced Indians, and the military command at San Carlos was incensed over the interpretation of the court's action as a pardon, especially for the murderer of Lieutenant Mott. The legal officer from the post, Lieutenant F. B. Fowler, appeared before the justice of the peace in Globe, Arizona Territory, and swore out a warrant for the arrest of Nah-diez-az, charging him with Mott's murder. On June 5, 1889, the arrest warrant was delivered to Gila county sheriff Glenn Reynolds for service, and once again Nah-diez-az surrendered without incident. He was given his preliminary hearing at Globe on June 21 and was held to answer at the October term of the territorial district court. Seventeen other Indian criminals soon joined him in jail, some by force and others by trickery, and among them was the notorious Apache Kid. One by one all the Indians were tried, convicted, and brought before the bench for sentencing, and all received sentences ranging from years in prison to life, all to be served at the territorial prison near Yuma. When the trial began for Nah-diez-az, the prosecution called Frank Porter, F. B. Fowler, Al Seiber, and Dr. Davis. Nah-diez-az was the only witness for his defense and he repeated the same story he had told at his first trial two years earlier, describing his threatened relocation by the military to a poorer patch of ground and the difficulties he had experienced in keeping the small patch of ground his family had owned for most of his life. He claimed that Porter and Mott had come armed, intending to evict him by force, and he only fired in self-defense. He testified that he had not intended to shoot Lieutenant Mott but had fired at Porter and missed. His defense attorney, Van Wagenen, then delivered a touching plea for mercy, emphasizing that Mott's death was more a tragedy than a murder. Nevertheless, the jury convicted Nah-diez-az of first-degree murder and on October 30, 1889, Judge J. H. Kibbey read the sentence:

You, Nah-diez-az, have been duly convicted in this court of a crime of murder. It is therefore considered and adjudged by this court that you, Nah-diez-az, suffer death. At a time to be hereafter appointed, not less than thirty nor more than sixty days from the date hereof, you shall be taken by the Sheriff of this county to a place within the walls or yard of the jail of this county and there be hanged by the neck until you are dead according to law. The Sheriff of this county is charged with the execution of this judgment.

Nah-diez-az was shocked at the death sentence and tried to interrupt the judge by crying out, "No! Me good Indian," but Sheriff Reynolds ordered him to be quiet so that the judge could finish the sentencing. Once Nah-diez-az was back in his jail cell, all the Indians discussed the various sentences they had received. Nah-diez-az, who had become familiar with the conditions at the territorial prison near Yuma, stated that death was the more lenient sentence, and the others agreed.

Five Apache Indians had been sentenced to hang at Florence: Chief Gon-sha, As-ki-say-la-ha, Pah-ala-gos-za, Kah-dos-la, and Na-con-qui-say. Sheriff Jere Fryer decided to do away with the usual trapdoor gallows and instead use a twitch-up arrangement, where the condemned man would stand on the ground and a great weight would drop and jerk him upward, breaking his neck. On Wednesday night, December 4, three of the Indians committed suicide, leaving only Kah-dos-la and Na-con-qui-say to hang two days later. Gila county sheriff Jerry Ryan, who had to hang Nah-diez-az in three weeks, attended and examined every detail of the gallows and preparations, and he was determined to follow the same pattern of execution. He had the twitch-up gallows erected in the jail yard during the afternoon hours of Christmas day, but he replaced the 1,700 pounds of quicksilver with a 340-pound copper bullion ingot, wrapped in chains and held aloft nearly nine feet above the ground with a stout rope. The hanging rope was passed over two pulleys on the overhead beam, with the end opposite the noose attached to the ingot. December 27 was as dark and gloomy as December 6 had been, and Father Monfort, who had consoled the Indians at Florence, had come to Globe for the same purpose. Father Monfort and Reverend N. F. Norton, of the Globe M. E. Church, tried to give Nah-diez-az religious comfort, but he was indifferent to their consolation. The day before his execution, he had asked Deputy Charles Miller the difference between Heaven and Earth. The deputy had told him that "Earth is Hell!" and this satisfied him. The condemned man's father had asked to visit the prisoner, but Nah-diez-az refused to see him, so he had no personal visitors as he awaited his death.

A twitch-up gallows with a copper ingot hovering above Nah-diez-az
PHOTO COURTESY OF THE ARIZONA HISTORICAL SOCIETY/ TUCSON; AHS# 60051

The prisoner slept well that night, and even the early arrival of official witnesses did not disturb him. At 8:00 a.m. Deputy T. A. Lonergan read the death warrant, with Indian interpreter Constant Bread translating, and this took a half hour. J. C. Lundy then cut the shackles, which Nah-diez-az had worn to prevent his escape during the weeks he spent in the jail, from the prisoner's ankles, and he danced about his cell once his ankles were freed. A few minutes before 9:00 a.m., it was time to make their way to the gallows, so the prisoner said good-bye to the Indian prisoners being held in the Globe jail while awaiting transfer to the prison at Yuma or awaiting trial. He was led into the jail yard, where he took his place on the low platform a few inches above the ground and stood directly

beneath the noose. Father Monfort, persistent to the last, tied a crucifix around Nah-diez-az's neck and carefully positioned it "upon the
victim's breast to illumine the way to eternity," and the priest then
recited a prayer. While the priest performed his functions, Deputy
Miller applied the straps to the prisoner's knees and ankles, wrists
and arms. Once the priest concluded, Nah-diez-az was asked if he
had anything to say, and he yelled out "Good-bye, Hell!" in reference
to Miller's explanation of Heaven and Earth. When it was apparent the condemned man had nothing further to say, Miller pulled
the black hood over the prisoner's head and adjusted and cinched
the noose in place. At 9:03 Deputy D. A. Reynolds took one swing
at the restraining rope and the copper ingot dropped. Nah-diez-az,
being short and light of weight, was jerked up with such force that
his head struck the crossbeam, crushing his skull. He dropped to the
end of the rope with a jerk, and there was a momentary twitching
of his fingers, a slight contraction of his limbs, and a single tremor
throughout his body, his toes dangling inches above the platform.
In seven minutes Dr. Largent, who monitored his vital signs, pronounced the prisoner dead, and he was cut down and put in the
cheap coffin provided by the county. That afternoon Nah-diez-az,
the first man legally hanged in Pinal County, was buried in Potter's
Field next to the graves of Curtis Hawley and Lafayette Grimes, who
had been lynched on August 24, 1882, for the murders of Andy Hall
and Dr. Vail.

CHAPTER 6

Virginia City's Iron Bridge Gallows

Thirty-one-year-old Louis Ortiz, alias Louis Bravo, was reportedly born near Tucson, Arizona, in 1860. Though he was often characterized as a "Spaniard," in his final moments he claimed his family lived in Mexico. He made his debut as a "bold, bad man" in Los Angeles, California, where he had a disagreement with a Negro and "cut him all to pieces." As soon as he got out of that scrape, he went to Cedarville, California, where he was employed by Dr. W. H. Patterson as a vaquero. While in this employment he built upon his reputation by carving up three men in separate knife fights, and he was involved in two shooting scrapes where no one was killed. Though he was not facing arrest or prosecution, Ortiz felt it best to leave that region, so he made his way to Winnemucca, Nevada, where he got into another cutting scrape, seriously wounded his adversary, and was driven out of town as an "undesirable" in the fall of 1889. Ortiz next went to Reno, Nevada, where his previous employer had settled. He wasted little time getting involved in another "carving bee" with Louis Melendez at the Russ House, but no charges were filed because it was determined to be mutual combat. Then, in June 1891, he took a shot at Denny Mann behind the Palace Hotel but failed to hit his mark. He was arrested and jailed, and he paid a small fine for discharging his weapon within the city limits before he was released. Ortiz's next offense involved another cutting scrape at Davis's saloon behind the

Palace Hotel where, on July 6, he fought with three men, but two fled when he bested them. Ortiz beat his remaining adversary, Gus Benois, over the head, knocking him senseless. Then he cut off one of his ears, carved him badly, and left him for dead. When Benois staggered onto the street from the alley, he was found by Officer Campbell, who summoned a doctor and then began to search for Ortiz. Benois was taken to a hospital, where he recovered, and Ortiz was soon arrested, brought before Judge J. J. Linn, and bound over for the grand jury on a charge of assault with intent to kill. However, District Attorney T. V. Julien concluded that the evidence was not sufficient to convict Ortiz on that charge, dismissed the case, and had the prisoner re-arrested on a simple assault charge; the defendant appeared before Judge Linn again, who fined him seventy-five dollars. Friends quickly paid his fine, and he was released with the understanding that he would leave Reno immediately and not return.

Ortiz went to Soda Springs, Nevada, and kept himself out of trouble, or at least did not commit any offenses that led to an arrest, and he remained for two months. He returned to Reno on September 17 on the 10:00 p.m. train and was told by friends that he had better "jump the town or you will be arrested," and he replied, "I would like to see any s_ of a b_ officer try to arrest me." Ortiz spent the rest of that evening at the bar in the Grand Central Hotel, where he drank freely until midnight, and then the bartender gave him a bed in the storeroom to sleep it off. However, Ortiz refused to stay in bed and kept returning to the saloon, which was crowded with guests. Dan O'Keefe cleared the barroom and Ortiz went out with the others, but when he reached the front porch Ortiz drew a pistol and, without provocation, began firing indiscriminately at various people. His first bullet grazed Tom Welch on his hip. He fired his second shot as bartender Thomas McCormack and night watchman Richard "Uncle Dick" Nash attempted to disarm him. This bullet struck Nash in the abdomen, and Nash later reported that he was certain it was intended. Though he was badly wounded, Nash persisted in his efforts to arrest Ortiz. Ortiz was finally subdued and disarmed by McCormack, but he broke free and ran down the street. McCormack chased and tackled Ortiz and held him down until Nash and O'Keefe arrived and arrested him. Ortiz was lodged alone in the smaller of two jail cells because in the larger cell was Baptiste, a bad Mexican with whom Ortiz previously had a disagreement. It was later suggested that if there had been no interference months earlier when these two were about to engage in a gun battle, they would have killed each other "and rid the country of two bad men."

Nash had arrived in Virginia City, Nevada, in 1863. By the 1870s he had prospected and mined all over Humboldt County, and he was elected sheriff of that county in 1874. When his term concluded he moved his family to Reno, where he served as town watchman. Nash was highly respected so it was not surprising that his shooting caused great outrage among Reno's citizens. Because of his wound, Nash was taken to his home and a doctor was summoned. After examining the officer, Dr. J. A. Lewis called in two other doctors for consultation. Doctors Dawson H. Bergstein and W. H. Patterson agreed that the bullet had probably not punctured his stomach, which would surely have proven fatal from infection in those early days of medicine. However, the doctors waited and watched for any complication that might develop, and it appeared for several days that Nash lay near death. The people of Reno prematurely mourned the death of their town watchman, and the newspapers published short eulogies, saving the longer articles postmortem. But Nash surprised everyone, rallied, and recovered from his wound, though the bullet remained in him throughout his life. By September 25 he was out of bed and "reportedly doing nicely and would soon be out and about the town." Within a month he was back on the job and continued in that position until he retired in 1902. On December 15, 1905, "Uncle Dick" Nash died at Reno at the age of sixty-eight.

As Nash "lay on his death bed" on the evening of September 18, a vigilance committee met at the lumberyard to consider what should be done with Ortiz. After considerable discussion it was unanimously agreed that he should hang. The committee sent out men as lookouts to keep the committee members abreast of any developments at the jail, and other men were sent to monitor Nash's condition. The main body of the committee waited until 11:45 p.m. before they made their march to the courthouse, where the jail was located. Shortly after midnight three men moved stealthily down Second Street and then Virginia Street to reconnoiter the area. At the corner of the photo gallery, seventy-five armed citizens, masked with handkerchiefs over their faces, gathered in the bright light of a full moon. Their leader moved into the corridors leading to the sheriff's office, followed by his committee, and he knocked on the door. Undersheriff John Caughlin asked, "Who is there?" and the man replied, "A friend who wants to see you." The undersheriff opened the office door and immediately faced a dozen revolvers. Caughlin was shoved into a chair and disarmed, and his pockets were searched for keys to the cells, but they were not found. The undersheriff was then ordered to open the jail door, but he said, "I quit right there. I will not open it." Caughlin was then convinced that it was no use to resist, so he gave up the keys, and the leader of the vigilance committee opened the jail door. Next they ordered Caughlin to open the inner door, which he did, and he was asked which cell Ortiz was in. He told them the prisoner was in the second cell, and the leader of the committee opened the door and called out, "Louis Ortiz, come out!" but Ortiz would not cooperate. The leader again asked which of the two cells Ortiz was in, and Caughlin told him "the smaller cell." Several of the vigilantes then went into the cell and told Ortiz, "Get up, you are wanted downtown." The prisoner replied, "All right," and walked out of his cell.

The vigilantes marched Ortiz out of the jail, leaving an armed guard to watch Caughlin. Ortiz's wrists were quickly tied behind his back and, with a man on each side, one in front, and several immediately behind, all with cocked revolvers pointed at his head, Ortiz was marched onto the iron bridge on Virginia Street. A double row of men was formed around the prisoner, and guards were placed at each end of the bridge to ensure there would be no interruption. The condemned man was given an opportunity to speak to the crowd, and he asked for a priest and a drink of water. Neither request could be complied with, but a whiskey flask was offered, and Ortiz drank deeply from its contents. After he handed back the flask, his arms were bound to his body and his ankles were bound. The noose was tightened about his neck and the opposite end was strung over a high beam. He was then given another opportunity to speak, and he gave a few directions as to his personal effects, insisted his real name was Louis Bravo, and requested that certain letters be written to his family in Mexico.

Ortiz was carefully positioned beneath the iron beam and asked if he was ready, and he replied, "Ready!" and the leader said, "Haul away!" At the command the rope quickly tightened, Ortiz's body rose and swayed, his head turned to one side with a quick jerk, and he was swung clear of the ground. He had hardly risen three feet when the rope snapped, and he fell backward onto the bridge. Ortiz was pulled up onto his feet and supported, and he had "a rather sickly smile" on his face as he pleaded with them to hurry, so one of the vigilantes rushed away and quickly returned with a rope with a larger diameter. A noose was tied and adjusted about Ortiz's neck, and at exactly 12:39 a.m. the condemned man was pulled up a second time and suspended from the beam of the iron bridge. The loose end of the rope was tied off as Ortiz's body swung and twisted about, followed by an occasional convulsion, and he was left hanging when the committee departed after all signs of life had ceased.

Virginia City's Iron Bridge, where Louis Ortiz was lynched
PHOTO COURTESY OF NEVADA HISTORICAL SOCIETY

During the early morning hours of September 19, coroner J. V. Peers and undertaker William Sanders were summoned to remove the body to the morgue. They arrived at 4:30 a.m. and found the body still suspended. They cut Ortiz down, left the noose in place for the inquest that was to follow, and placed him in a coffin in the undertaker's wagon bed. The body was driven to the town morgue, and coroner Peers called for an inquest jury. He impaneled Calvin Conn, W. M. Anderson, J. E. Campbell, John Frazer, W. A. Wimer, and John Horne, who found:

We, the undersigned, the jurors summoned to appear before coroner Peers at Reno, Saturday, September 19, 1891 to inquire into the cause of death of a man named Louis Ortiz, having been duly sworn according to the law, and having made some inquisition after inspecting the body, and hearing the testimony adduced, upon our oath each and all do say, that the deceased was named Louis Ortiz, was a native of Mexico, aged about 31 or 32 years, and that he came to his death on the morning of September 19th, 1891, in this township and county, by means of a rope around his neck by unknown parties to us. All of which we duly certify by this requisition in writing by us undersigned this 19th day of September, A. D., 1891.

It is interesting to note that the jurors found Ortiz a native Mexican, which had only been confirmed at the time of his lynching to the members of the lynching party. Ortiz was buried in the Catholic cemetery that same day.

Nine days later, on September 28, Judge Cheney addressed the Washoe County grand jury at length on the subject of unpunished murder. He said that the lynching of Ortiz "was in no way justified, right, or seemly. The only established means of determining guilt or innocence has been supplanted by a body of unknown, unauthorized, irrepressible, and self-constituted lynchers." He called the hanging of Ortiz a murder, but his motivation for this harangue may have been a comment in the article detailing the lynching in which the *Reno Evening Gazette* blamed "the slow and tardy process of justice, as administered in the courts of law."

CHAPTER 7

The Tramp Murderer

Early on Saturday, August 13, 1892, two tramps arrived in Missoula, Montana, on an eastbound freight train. John Burns and a man who called himself Lyons, but whose real name was Gannon, spent nearly all their time at the gaming tables, and by the evening of the following day they had lost nearly all their money. Burns tried to pawn a watch at one of the prominent saloons, but he was turned away. Sometime shortly after midnight, while a fire raged in town, Lyons tried to sell a valuable ring to Paul Goldenbogen, but the potential buyer thought the ring might have been stolen and had Lyons arrested by Officer Blendour so it could be investigated. At 4:00 a.m. Goldenbogen was standing in front of the Exchange Saloon when John Burns approached and asked why he had informed on Lyons. As Goldenbogen was answering, Burns pulled out a pistol and shot him, the bullet striking Goldenbogen in his right side. The wounded man reeled toward the front of the sidewalk, where Maurice Higgins, Frank Smith, and Tom Black were standing. The three men turned at the sound of the gunshot, and, as they looked at Burns, he fired again. The second bullet struck Higgins a little to one side of the center of his forehead, and Higgins fell on his face on the sidewalk. Goldenbogen exclaimed, "I am shot, too!" and fell across Higgins's body.

Maurice Higgins, brother of Missoula's Mayor Frank G. Higgins, was just a boy, but he was a member of the town's fire department. On the evening of August 14, he had been on the front line fighting a terrible fire that had started at the rear of the Blue Front Saloon on Front Street. Before the flames were extinguished, the conflagration had consumed the Rogers Hotel, Hawkes' Stable, and a dozen other buildings. After battling the fire for hours, Higgins joined two fellow firemen to discuss their success in stopping the further spread of the fire, and that was the only reason young Higgins was standing in front of the Exchange Saloon at that early hour.

After firing the second shot, Burns ran eastward with Tom Black in close pursuit, but the tramp waved his pistol at his pursuer and threatened Black, who was unarmed, so he had to let Burns escape. However, he watched Burns run to the corner of the Hammond block and turn toward the bridge over the Clark Fork River. Sheriff William Houston quickly arrived on the scene and took up the chase by following Black's directions. When the sheriff reached the bridge, he saw Burns at the other end, but when he got to the other side of the river he lost sight of the fugitive near the baseball park. He searched the area but could find no sign of Burns, so he started back toward town. When he got to the bridge again he saw Burns, this time crossing back into town, and he began his pursuit again. When the sheriff was at the center of the north span, he saw Burns passing the Hammond block, now in the opposite direction from earlier. Once across the bridge the sheriff saw the fugitive, still some distance away, enter the Concordia Saloon but immediately exit. Black joined the sheriff and positively identified the man being chased as the shooter, and together they followed Burns around the corner onto Main Street, caught up with Burns two doors west of the *Missoulian* newspaper office, and arrested him without resistance. He had no gun on his person and it was never found, so it was supposed he had thrown it into the river while on the bridge, either going or coming. Meanwhile, Higgins had been carried to the family residence immediately after being shot and two surgeons carefully cut into his skull to extract the bullet, but they could not find it. The doctors claimed that the wound would have been immediately fatal to most men, but young Higgins's strength and vitality sustained him for nearly twelve hours until he died at 3:30 p.m.

Goldenbogen was taken to Sister's Hospital, where he had recovered sufficiently by 11:30 a.m. to have a brief visit. Sheriff Houston brought Burns to the hospital, and the wounded man positively identified him as the one who shot him and Higgins. Burns fainted when brought face-to-face with his initial victim. Soon after Burns was returned to his cell, Higgins died and the prisoner was charged with his murder. John Burns then claimed his real name was Hugh J. Hamilton and he had been born in New York State in 1859. His father was a stationary engineer in a small village there, and he had four brothers and three sisters. He said that at seventeen years of age he left home and started wandering the West, but he was heading east when he and Lyons stopped at Missoula. He and Lyons, in adjacent cells, then began to concoct their defense.

Burns was indicted and arraigned on the murder charge. His trial was set for September 12 in Judge Marshall's courtroom, beginning with two days of jury selection and followed by two days of testimony. The defendant was positively identified by Sheriff Houston and by Charles Moore, the night bartender at the Headquarters Saloon, as well as by Smith and Black. Goldenbogen was brought in on a stretcher and he identified the defendant as the man who had shot him and murdered Higgins, but under the strain of testifying the witness began to suffer hemorrhaging. It was thought he would die in the courtroom; he was rushed back to Sister's Hospital, where he rallied and fully recovered. The sheriff then took the jury on an excursion to the bridge and walked them across and down to the baseball park, emphasizing various points along the way where the pursuit had evolved, but the defendant was kept under guard on the town side of the bridge. Back in the courtroom Burns's defense was that the sheriff had arrested the

John Burns
DAILY MISSOULIAN: DECEMBER 16, 1892

wrong man and his partner was named Haywick, not Lyons, so he had no motive for the shooting. He said that he and Haywick had been watching the fire during the early hours of the conflagration but then went to a house of ill fame and had just left when they heard two shots fired some distance away. Lyons, still in jail, was brought in and he testified that his partner was named Brown, not Burns, and that it was Brown who had shot Higgins. However, the mysterious Brown and Haywick were conspicuously absent in court, as were the sporting ladies Burns claimed to have been with during the murder.

The case went to the jury during the afternoon of September 16, and by 10:00 p.m. they had found Burns guilty of first-degree murder. On September 20 Judge Marshall sentenced Burns to hang on November 11, 1892. On October 5 Burns's attorney filed a motion for a new trial based upon the error that during the excursion to the bridge his client had been excluded from being present while evidence was presented to the jury. The motion was sustained on October 12, and a second trial was ordered. Burns's second trial commenced on October 17 and lasted ten days. Although it was a much longer trial, the evidence was substantially the same. The jury retired after 4:00 p.m. on October 27, and at 5:05 p.m. the following day Burns was again found guilty of first-degree murder. Judge Marshall, on November 5, sentenced Burns to hang on December 16, 1892. Neither appeal nor petition to Governor Joseph Toole, praying for a commutation of sentence, delayed the execution.

The gallows was erected well in advance of the date. It was the same gallows, with some modifications to the trapdoor, used to hang four Indians two years earlier: Antley, La-la-see, Pascale, and Pierre Paul; the hangman's rope was the same used to hang Pierre Paul. As for the gallows itself, two upright pieces were mortised into a crosspiece lying upon the ground; at the top, fifteen feet from the lower crosspiece, was another crosspiece mortised and bolted into the uprights. The bottom of each upright was braced about three feet from the ground. Adjoining the two main uprights were two other solid uprights holding the platform seven feet above the lower crosspiece on the ground. The outer part of this platform was a trapdoor, about three feet by two feet, attached by iron hinges and held up by a stout rope passing through pulleys on each of the lesser uprights, and when the rope was severed the trap would fall. Twelve steps led to the platform, and on the second step from the top was a button, which the sheriff would activate with his foot to sever the rope and spring the trapdoor. The drop was set at seven feet. This entire contraption was built within a high enclosure, and on the eastern side was a door that connected, through an enclosed passageway, to the east door of the jail.

Soon after Burns was convicted, he contemplated suicide when he found a packet of morphine left by the previous occupant of his cell. He considered taking a lethal dose but lost his nerve and handed over the narcotic to the jailor. As the day of his execution approached, his thoughts turned to escape, and he had one of his many visitors pass him a fine-toothed saw and a packet of a sleeping drug. A close watch had been placed on Burns after his first conviction, and it was kept up, with Al Weinrich assigned during the day and "old man" Nobles at night. It was the habit of Nobles to eat supper at midnight and wash it down with a glass of water from a pitcher that stood on a stand in the room. On Tuesday, December 13, shortly after eating his supper, Nobles began to feel unusually drowsy. He fought off the sleepiness as long as he could but finally dozed off. Burns then started sawing at the lock of the cell door, but Sheriff Houston was a very light sleeper and awoke at the slight but peculiar noise. The sheriff's quarters in the jail were adjacent to Burns's cell, and he hurried into the jail proper to investigate. Burns heard the sheriff coming and hid the saw blade but kept the handle to make it seem as if he had thrown the blade out of the window. Burns was then moved to a regular cell at the front of the jail and guarded by another deputy until Weinrich came on duty at his regular hour. When Nobles finally awoke the following morning, he was very sick for a time, vomiting freely from the effects of the drug. After Weinrich relieved the substitute deathwatch guard, he returned to search Burns's cell and found hidden in the broom the nine-inch saw blade with teeth on both edges, and Nobles was replaced on deathwatch duty.

After the failed attempt to escape, Burns admitted he had been angry with the sheriff and one of his deputies but said he no longer held a grudge over their part in his arrest and two convictions. He told a deputy, "You can't blame me for trying to escape. It was a matter of life and death with me and, of course, I would take all chances to escape." A reporter visited Burns during the day, learned nothing new about the crime or escape attempt, but was invited back in the evening. At 7:00 p.m. Burns was shaved by barber Simpson and half an hour later the reporter was admitted to the cell, but Burns again had nothing new to say. The condemned man had sent for Mayor Higgins, and the brother of the murdered boy expected a confession or at least a plea for forgiveness, but by the time he arrived Burns had changed his mind and would say nothing. Burns had previously said a person, whose identity he would not divulge, would avenge upon the mayor his death upon the gallows, but he told the mayor he did not want revenge and would try to have it stopped, as it had been a bluff that had no effect. At 10:00 p.m. all the prisoners were locked in their cells and were soon asleep, indifferent to the fate of fellow prisoner Burns.

On the night before his execution, Burns would eat nothing when provided food at 10:30 p.m. At midnight he refused to sleep. At 1:00 a.m. he again refused to eat but half an hour later requested whiskey, which was denied. From 2:00 to 3:30 a.m., the prisoner talked incessantly but said little of importance and nothing new, then he finally retired and was asleep in half an hour. The condemned man awoke at 6:00 a.m. and ate several oranges, which gave him an appetite, so he ate a hearty breakfast soon afterward. At 9:00 a.m. the *Missoulian* reporter returned, and within minutes they were joined by Father Guidi, who had been Burns's religious advisor for weeks. The priest administered communion and conferred the acts of contrition and faith, hope, and charity. At 9:30 a.m. Al Weinrich gave Burns a drink of whiskey. The prisoner requested to walk to the scaffold with a cigar in his mouth, and it was provided. At 9:40 Deputy Woods escorted the prisoner throughout the jail so that he could say good-bye to the other prisoners, and then Sheriff Houston read the death warrant to the prisoner in the jail corridor. With the fatal hour finally at hand, the procession formed and Burns was marched into the jail yard and onto the gallows, slightly assisted by Father Guidi.

Once on the platform Burns turned to the small crowd of witnesses and said, "Well, boys, I bid you farewell." Sheriff Houston slipped the noose over Burns's head and adjusted it under his left ear before cinching it in place, and next the straps were quickly applied to his wrists and arms, knees and ankles. Father Guidi, to distract him while this work was being done, talked to the condemned man of eternity, and Burns responded to the priest, "Oh Christ, be my savior! Oh, Christ, be my savior!" Sheriff Houston asked, "Jack, is there anything more you wish to say?" and he replied loudly, "No, let her go!" but then added in a low tone, "Make a good job of it, Bill." The black hood was quickly pulled over Burns's head and the attendants retired from the platform, the sheriff being the last to leave. When the sheriff stepped onto the first step, he hesitated for a moment and then gave a short kick to the trigger. There was a rattle as the trigger was pulled, the rope was cut, and the trapdoor was sprung. The condemned man broke his neck in the seven-foot fall, but there were two slight heaves of his chest before his body hung motionless. Doctors Billmyer and Fitzgerald monitored vital signs, and eleven minutes after the prisoner stepped onto the trapdoor they pronounced Burns dead. They let the body hang a sufficient time to ensure he could not be revived, and then the body was cut down and placed in a coffin provided by the county. The body was taken to Flynn's undertaking parlor, and at 2:00 p.m. the following day Burns was buried in the Catholic cemetery following a service by Father Guidi.

CHAPTER 8

Overcome by His Lust!

Albert F. Bomberger was born on February 18, 1871. At age seventeen he left his home in Lebanon City, Pennsylvania, and began working his way west. In December 1892 he arrived at the Krieder farm southeast of Cando in Towner County, in present-day North Dakota. He was hired as a farmhand by Daniel Kreider and treated as part of the family, even being given a bedroom on the second floor of the house, where Mr. and Mrs. Krieder's eight children also had their rooms. The oldest was a pretty fifteen-year-old girl named Annie, and Bomberger soon became hopelessly infatuated with her. When he could not control his lust, he made several indecent proposals, which Annie refused. On July 4, while drinking heavily, he formed a plan to visit Annie's bedroom on the evening of July 6. He carried out his plan after midnight but was scornfully rejected once again. This time, because of his persistence, Annie threatened to call her parents, who slept on the first floor. Bomberger retreated to his room, located next to Annie's bedroom, to sulk over being rebuffed. On the morning of July 7, as the farmhand began his chores, he resolved that he would murder the entire Krieder family and outrage Annie.

After brooding over the situation for a brief period, Bomberger went into the house, took a double-barreled shotgun and shells, and went looking for Daniel. He found his benefactor asleep in his bedroom and shot him full of buckshot from one barrel. He next went into the kitchen, where Mrs. Krieder was preparing breakfast, and shot her to death. He proceeded up the stairs from the kitchen to the childrens' rooms and ordered Annie, twelve-year-old Aaron, five-year-old Eva, and three-year-old Henry into his room while he went about his work. He next shot the eleven-year-old girl named Merby. Mary, who was nine years old, and seven-year-old David were shot next with a single load of buckshot fired into each child. Bernice, a thirteen-year-old girl, jumped from a second-story window and ran to the barn, but Bomberger followed. He intended to kill her there, but she begged so piteously to see her family again that he dragged her back into the house and let her see each dead body. As Bernice looked over the bodies of her brother and sisters, Bomberger noticed that Mary, the second child he had shot, was still alive, so he took a butcher knife and cut her throat. Then, as Bernice crouched in a corner on the second floor, her hands thrown over her face in a futile defensive gesture, he shot her dead from close range.

Bomberger then took Annie to her room and raped her, leaving the other three children in his room. While the murderer was preoccupied, Aaron, Eva, and Henry escaped and hid among the farm buildings, but, after raping Annie, Bomberger had lost interest in killing them. Instead, he dragged Annie to the barn and raped her again, then ordered her to the house to make his breakfast. He saddled his pony before he went into the kitchen, but he had lost his appetite and could not eat. He forced Annie to hand over fifty dollars of the family's funds, all she could find, and ordered her to pack a lunch for him. He herded Annie back to the barn, where he forced her into a loft, bound her, and then fled north toward the international border. Annie was freed by the other children after the murderer rode off, and she walked into Cando to report the crime.

Sheriff John "Jack" McCune of Towner County started out on Bomberger's trail alone. He overtook and captured the murderer

Sheriff Barton

DAILY PLAINDEALER: JANUARY 19, 1894

without resistance at Deloraine, Manitoba, Canada, on July 8 and brought his prisoner across the border without extradition papers. A large number of Cando's residents were intent upon lynching Bomberger, so Sheriff McCune eluded them at Cando. With the assistance of Sheriff Barton of Ramsey County, he instead took his prisoner by way of Barton's county seat of Devil's Lake into Grand Forks in Grand Forks County, where Sheriff Fadden lodged the prisoner in his jail. A contingent of Cando residents then started for Grand Forks for the same purpose, so Sheriff Fadden, to prevent further bloodshed, decided to remove his prisoner to Fargo. However, when he got to the Winnipeg Junction, he learned that the "mob" consisted of only nineteen prominent citizens of Towner County, so he returned his prisoner to the jail at Grand Forks.

In November Bomberger was returned to Cando to stand trial. The party left Grand Forks in a special car on the St. John train and passed through Devils Lake, where a crowd had gathered but made no demonstration. At Churchs Ferry, the lawmen and their prisoner took a wagon the last seventeen miles into Cando. Upon arriving in town Sheriff McCune took his prisoner to the Congregational Church. Avoiding a large crowd, Bomberger had his preliminary hearing before a justice of the peace. The next morning, November 21, the grand jury met and returned six indictments for murder in the first degree. Bomberger was held under close guard in a small room above the church so he would not have to be transported through the streets of Cando, and the church was to be used for the trial because the courtroom could not hold the large number of spectators expected. The prisoner was brought down before noon to have the indictments read, and the trial began at 1:30 p.m. The murderer was only charged with the killings of Bernice and Mary at this first trial, as these were considered the strongest cases of premeditation. Bomberger had no attorney, so J. O'Brien of Devils Lake was appointed to represent the defendant and the court recessed for one hour. The court reconvened at 2:35 p.m. and Bomberger pled guilty, possibly hoping to avoid the death penalty by cooperating, and the entire proceeding took only fifteen minutes. The district attorney then asked Judge David Morgan to allow him to call the county coroner to testify to the postmortem examinations, to enlighten the judge as to the enormity of the crimes, and after this testimony concluded the court adjourned until 5:00 p.m. on Thursday, November 23. The court reconvened a few minutes after 4:00 p.m., and Judge Morgan asked the defendant, "Have you any cause why sentence should not be passed upon you at this time?" When Bomberger answered, "No, sir," the judge continued, "The crime is an atrocious one, the annals of crime reveal none worse. The court discovers no reason for clemency; that the sentence of this court is that you are to be hanged by the neck until you are dead, and may God have mercy on your soul." He then set the date of execution for January 19, 1894.

The scaffold was erected by Scotsman Elmer Judd in a small meadow one mile north of Cando, a half mile north of the Shanley Slaughter House and adjoining the William McDonald place on the east, just north of the road running east and west between sections 17 and 20. This place was chosen because the elevated ground surrounding the meadow provided a good view for any who desired to witness the execution. Judd claimed to have built several gallows in Scotland before coming to North Dakota, and his work reflected his knowledge and skill. The scaffold was contained within a fence seven feet high enclosing an area twenty-four feet square, more to hold back the crowd than to obstruct their view, as the platform of the gallows was visible above the top of the fence. From that platform the condemned man, if he chose to look, could plainly see the Krieder farmhouse. The hanging rope had arrived on Christmas day and was made of hemp, half an inch in diameter and one hundred feet in length.

The prisoner was kept in a room on the second floor of the courthouse, where a mattress on the floor served as a bed for Bomberger. Three deathwatch guards were with him constantly because there were no bars on the courthouse windows. The prisoner spent his days playing cards and smoking his pipe; he maintained a hearty appetite, and he slept "as peacefully each night as a man whose mind is at ease with himself and all mankind." On the day before his execution, Bomberger remarked to the sheriff, "I wish I had not pled guilty." Sheriff McCune answered, "You've got no kick coming, Bomberger. You were given a chance to plead and plenty of time to think about it before hand." Bomberger thought for a moment and then replied, "Yes, I know what you say is so, and I have no kick coming on the way I was used, and the show given me. It would probably have been the same thing in the end, yet I cannot help wishing that I had pled 'not guilty.'"

During his final days many women visited, mostly the curious but also several sympathizers, but the condemned man was too much taken up with his own thoughts to pay them much attention. Newsmen began to arrive in town on January 17 and several tried, but failed, to get an interview with the prisoner. On the morning of the execution, a representative of the *Fargo Forum* requested to photograph Bomberger, but the condemned man objected. He ate a hearty dinner at noon, and

Albert Bomberger hanged
PHOTO COURTESY OF THE NORTH DAKOTA STATE UNIVERSITY

then smoked his pipe until Sheriff McCune came at 12:45 p.m. with a bowl of water and a clean pair of socks. After bathing, Bomberger returned to his chair in the auditor's office, where the sheriff read the death warrant. Bomberger had nothing to say in response and refused the services of a clergyman, saying about his faith, "I do not know what I believe." The sheriff informed Bomberger that the time set for the execution, 1:30 p.m., was near at hand and that he should finish dressing, so the prisoner put on his vest and coat and walked out of the courthouse to the waiting sleigh. He took his seat between two county sheriffs and was driven into the enclosure surrounding the gallows. The prisoner was given an opportunity to shake hands with the official witnesses near the gallows and bid them farewell, then he walked up the stairs and took his place on the trapdoor, a vantage point from which he could see the crowd of more than one thousand spectators on the surrounding hills. Though the prisoner had refused to have his picture taken, a photographer set up his camera some distance from the gallows and snapped a picture of the execution. The only likeness of Bomberger was the sketch made by a member of a newspaper's art staff, and it appeared in the *Daily Globe* of St. Paul, Minnesota.

As soon as Bomberger was in place, Sheriff McCune quickly pinioned the prisoner's wrists and arms, knees and ankles and adjusted and cinched the noose in place. He then asked if the prisoner had anything to say. Bomberger responded in a loud, clear voice, "Gentlemen, I have a few words to say before I leave you. I committed the crime and am sorry for it, and I hope no one here will ever follow in my footsteps. I want no clergyman on the scaffold with me. Good-bye, all!" A persistent reverend, who had visited the prisoner in his room several times, called out, "Albert, look to Jesus!" and Bomberger replied only, "Thank you." The black hood was drawn over his head and with the words, "Good-bye, Jack; good-bye, Sheriff," the bolt was drawn and at 1:33 p.m. the trapdoor was sprung. Bomberger fell eight feet, the toes of his shoes clearing the ground by only six inches. There were three doctors in attendance, and they immediately stepped forward, announced that the prisoner's neck was broken, and recorded his pulse. In one minute it had elevated to 176 but fell rapidly until it was only 46 in six minutes. In eight minutes more, at 1:47 p.m., Bomberger's heart ceased to beat and he was pronounced dead. The body was cut down and placed in the cheap coffin provided by the county, then carried to the courthouse, where hundreds of curious citizens viewed the remains of the mass murderer. Bomberger was buried in the public cemetery one mile east of Cando at dusk. Later a telegram was received from his parents requesting that the body of their son be sent to Pennsylvania for final interment.

CHAPTER 9

A Double Twitch-up in Cañon City

On the morning of January 23, 1893, Thomas A. Jordan was fired from his day-shift job at the Omaha & Grant Smelter in Denver, Colorado. He went directly to a saloon at Fortieth and Market Streets and spent the afternoon drinking liquor. At 7:00 p.m., then drunk, Jordan left the saloon and returned to the smelter to find day foreman John Skilman. He had armed himself with a .38 caliber revolver "of a cheap pattern," which he concealed in his pocket. Believing that Skilman had dealt him a mortal insult in discharging him, Jordan told some of the workmen at the smelter he would "fill Skilman full of lead as soon as I meet him." Some of the men called night foreman Henry Dierstein, who asked Jordan, "What is the matter, my friend?" Jordan answered, "I am hunting for Skilman; you get away or I'll kill you." Dierstein stepped back, out of Jordan's path, and Jordan walked into a building that had just been erected in the yard. Watchman August Gisen was summoned next, and he was warned that Jordan was "acting in an ugly manner." Gisen, who knew Jordan, walked into the building and asked him, "You wouldn't shoot me, would you?" to which Jordan replied, "No, I wouldn't shoot anybody." As Jordan spoke he pulled his revolver from his pocket and shot Gisen. The bullet struck Gisen in the chest just above his heart, and the watchman collapsed. A doctor was summoned, but Gisen bled to death in two hours.

Immediately after the shot was fired, Jordan ran to the railroad tracks and hid in the freight cars, but two lawmen followed his trail and arrested the murderer before midnight. Jordan was lodged in jail, and at his examination he was held over for trial at the summer term of the court. Jordan was convicted of first-degree murder, and when Judge Rising pronounced the sentence of death in early July, Jordan shouted, "You damned old coward, it shows what a cur you are. If I had known this you would not have sentenced me." The court officers shackled the combative Jordan before they removed him from the courtroom. Jordan arrived at the penitentiary in Cañon City on July 14, 1893, and was registered as prisoner No. 3268. He was scheduled to hang during the week commencing July 23, but on July 20 Governor Davis H. Waite, who was opposed to the death penalty, granted a thirty-day respite so that defense attorney H. B. O'Reilly could file an appeal with the state's supreme court. O'Reilly's grounds were based upon a writ of error, and the court issued a supersedeas, which stayed the execution. The high court finally upheld the lower court's conviction and sentence, and the date for Jordan's execution was set for April 22, 1894. The governor then began issuing a series of thirty-, sixty-, and ninety-day respites until the case carried over into the term of newly elected Governor Albert W. McIntire. The new governor granted a sixty-day respite from March 3, 1895, when Governor Waite's last respite ended, so that the matter of Jordan's sanity could be resolved. He commissioned Drs. Joseph W. Thombs and John T. Eskridge to examine the prisoner, and they found that, while some of Jordan's behavior was markedly bizarre, the prisoner was sufficiently sane to be executed. Those who had continuous contact with the prisoner, particularly his deathwatch guards, insisted that his strange behavior was feigned and that he was perfectly normal when not under medical observation. The final respite had moved the date for Jordan's execution to the second week of May 1895, and a campaign then began to have the governor commute Jordan's sentence to life imprisonment. Petitions and visits to the governor from family members filled those final days, and the governor was occupied with the case until 5:00 p.m. on the day preceding Jordan's execution when he met with the justices of the state supreme court. The governor left their chambers firm in his resolve, and at 6:00 p.m. he gave notice that he was ready to hear H. B. O'Reilly's final plea. Jordan's sister, a pretty girl of twenty-

Thomas Jordan
SAN FRANCISCO CHRONICLE: MAY 12, 1895

five years, sat quietly throughout the presentation, which was based upon the contention that an information rather than an indictment deprived Jordan of due process. The state's supreme court justices had already found otherwise, citing a California case, so at the conclusion Governor McIntire refused to intervene.

Peter Agusta, an Italian of fifty-one years, was living next door to Mrs. Nellie Holmes at 1425 McNasser Avenue, Denver, and they had been engaged in an intimate relationship for some time. Agusta learned that Nellie had recently taken Harry Sullivan, whose real name was David McClennigan, as her lover, and on the afternoon of July 19, 1892, Agusta peered through a window and saw the pair drinking beer. He became uncontrollably jealous, rushed home, and chose a stiletto as his weapon of attack. He returned and waited until the couple retired, and then he crept into the house. Sullivan was in bed alone and lying on his right side asleep when Agusta plunged the blade into Sullivan's left side just behind his left armpit. Agusta struck a second time in Sullivan's back before the wounded man fled from the room while crying out for help. Sullivan reached the rear door, but he was already so weak from the loss of blood that he could barely turn the handle. Agusta followed closely and plunged the long stiletto blade into Sullivan's back once more before he fled. At 1:30 on the morning of July 20, Sullivan was found unconscious, lying on the blood-soaked ground at Nineteenth and Page Streets. He was rushed to the county hospital, where he was revived, made an antemortem statement, and died later that day.

The police had little to go on until Sullivan regained consciousness and gave his statement. Then the search for Agusta began in earnest, and the murderer was soon found and lodged in jail. At his examination Agusta was held over for trial, and he was tried in the criminal division of the district court. He claimed that the wounds had been inflicted with a pair of shears in self-defense, but the police surgeon testified that the wounds could not have been inflicted as Agusta described. The stiletto was never found. Testimony showed that Agusta had asked Mrs. Holmes to marry him, but she refused because her estranged husband lived near Denver. Her recent liaison with Sullivan, which resulted in the exclusion of Agusta from her bed, was believed to be his motive. Agusta was found guilty of first-degree murder on October 19 and was sentenced to hang in December 1892. On December 5 Governor John L. Routt granted a reprieve of thirty-five days, which delayed the execution until after Governor Waite took office. Waite, rather than commute Agusta's sentence, granted a series of reprieves as he had done for Jordan, the last of which ended March 8, 1895, after Governor McIntire took office. The newly elected governor then granted a reprieve of sixty days to look into the case but eventually declined to intervene. The date for the execution of Agusta was set for the second week of May, to coincide with the date set for Thomas Jordan's execution. Agusta did not have a good reputation, even among his own countrymen, but an effort was launched to obtain a commutation of sentence. The Italian consul was petitioned to use his influence to persuade the governor, but the consul investigated every detail of the affair and decided Agusta deserved his fate. Among the circumstances found was that Agusta had three previous mistresses, two of whom died in his house under circumstances that defied explanation, and the third was confined in the insane asylum at Pueblo.

Agusta was attended by Father Ferrari, to whom he gave his written dying statement:

I die innocent of the crime for which I am in a short time going to be executed by hanging. I stabbed the man whom I had never known before with a pair of scissors and not with a knife or stiletto, because he attacked me first, threatening death, and with open and avowed intent to rob me of part of the money that he knew I had on my person. I forgive all that had any part in my unjust conviction. May God forgive them.

Peter Agusta.

Agusta's last day and night were passed as calmly as any other during his long confinement, and he declined breakfast, saying he was fasting on religious grounds. His religious advisor was the first caller that last day, and the priest stayed with Agusta for an hour. The Reverend Father said later, "Agusta is fully resigned. He feels his death to be an ignominious one, but he knows that our Savior's was also, and he is courageous and cheerful in the knowledge that a better life awaits him. . . . To me the fact is established absolutely that Agusta is innocent of murder. I believe he killed the man in self-defense. The Governor, when I was before the pardon board, objected to my calling Agusta's execution a legal murder. I wrote Governor McIntire a letter yesterday

Peter Agusta
SAN FRANCISCO CHRONICLE: MAY 12, 1895

and put even a little more pepper into the emphasizing of that fact."

Doctor J. J. Dawson, the prison's physician, came next to examine the prisoner. Agusta was well enough but had remained most of the morning on his cot, covered with his blankets and engaged in prayer and meditation. He chatted with the doctor, who also found him perfectly resigned to his fate. The doctor also noted that Agusta was somewhat depressed, as he had no friends or relatives to visit while the man in the next cell, Thomas Jordan, had quite a large number of friends and family visiting him for several days. At noon Agusta ended his fast and ate a hearty dinner. He was alone until 2:00 p.m., except for his deathwatch guard, and spent the time in meditation until his priest arrived, and the clergyman was with Agusta almost constantly until the end.

The witnesses were then arriving in Cañon City, the last being Sheriff M. F. Bowers of El Paso County, who was to arrive at 7:00 p.m. to deliver a convict. As soon as all the witnesses entered the warden's office in the early evening, the prisoners in the general population were called in and locked in their cells. Fifty people had gathered outside the gate and, seeing the prisoners removed from the yard, had the impression that the execution was about to take place. This caused great excitement, but one of the guards explained that it was only the usual time for the prisoners' baths. The condemned men, according to law, had been kept in solitary confinement for thirty days prior to the first day of the week in which they were to be executed, and they could receive no visitors excepting a member of their family, one at a time, and their religious advisor. Once the condemned men were removed from solitary confinement to their death row cells, a deathwatch guard was posted within each cell twenty-four hours a day and a second guard paced the corridor day and night.

Thomas Jordan was scheduled to die first, so Agusta could wait only with his deathwatch guard. Jordan's brother, James, remained with Thomas until urged to leave, and after James left the prison the witnesses were brought into the death chamber. The doors to the cells of the two condemned men were covered by curtains while the witnesses were led from the warden's office through the weight room into the death chamber. Once the witnesses were in place, the curtains were removed and at 8:30 p.m. Warden John Cleghorn went to the cell of Jordan, where he read the death warrant and long history of respites. Straps were applied to the prisoner's wrists and arms, and he walked the short distance, about twenty-five feet, into the twenty-foot-by-twenty-foot execution room across the narrow corridor from the cells. He was escorted by two deputies and accompanied by his priest, who for the first time that afternoon had left the side of Agusta. Jordan, who had declined to speak to the witnesses, took his place in front of the platform, and straps were applied to his knees and ankles. The noose was adjusted by Warden Cleghorn, and the black hood was pulled over his head from behind. The two deputies then lifted the prisoner onto the platform, which activated the trigger of the "automatic suicide machine."

Noverto Griego had been the first man executed after the law was changed to require that condemned men be executed at the prison in Cañon City rather than in the county of conviction. A special building was erected in the northeast portion of the penitentiary yard. Inside

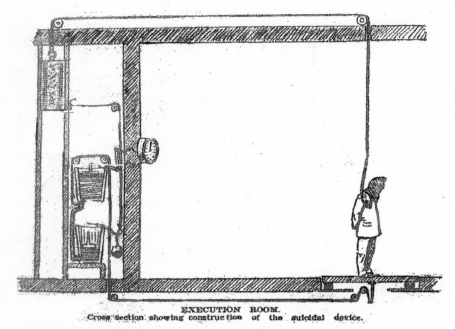

EXECUTION ROOM.
Cross section showing construction of the suicidal device.

The "automatic suicide machine" at Cañon City
ROCKY MOUNTAIN NEWS: MAY 12, 1895

were six cells for death row prisoners, and across a narrow corridor were three rooms. One contained an elaborate apparatus of buckets and weights and was called the weight room, the second was the twenty-foot-by-twenty-foot execution chamber, and the third room was used for storage, including the caskets for the deceased. When Griego was executed on November 8, 1890, the weight had to be dropped manually. Because this was a most distasteful duty, Deputy Warden George E. Dudley became determined to design a release that was activated by the weight of the condemned man—an automatic suicide machine. When the condemned was lifted onto the spring-loaded platform, his weight pulled a cord running beneath the floor, and this opened a valve in the weight room so that water from an upper bucket began draining into a lower bucket. When the twenty-nine pounds of water in the upper bucket was reduced to eleven pounds, the upper bucket shifted, pulling an iron rod that held up a twenty-five-pound iron ball; this, in turn, dropped and tripped a trigger holding aloft a 300-pound weight. The end opposite the noose in the hanging rope was attached to the heavy weight after running over pulleys on a beam above, and when the weight dropped the condemned was suddenly jerked upward, or "jerked to Jesus," hopefully breaking his neck by dislocating it between the first and second or second and third vertebrae. There was a float in the upper bucket, and as the water level dropped it recorded progress on a gauge on the wall of the execution chamber. It took ninety seconds from the time the prisoner was lifted onto the platform until the weight dropped and he was jerked to his death.

After Jordan was in place on the platform, all eyes, save those of the prisoner, turned to the gauge on the wall. When the 300-pound weight dropped to the floor in the room next to the death chamber, Jordan was jerked five feet into the air and then settled back until his toes were eighteen inches above the platform. Doctors F. M. Carrier and J. J. Dawson stepped forward and, each taking a wrist, counted Jordan's pulse. Jordan's legs were convulsively drawn up three times but quickly straightened. The pulse decreased for seven minutes and, in the eighth minute, only a quiver of the heart was perceptible. At 8:51 p.m. the doctors pronounced him dead and, after the body hung a few minutes more, Jordan's remains were lowered onto a stretcher and carried into the storage room. Jordan's neck had not been broken in the jerk, so he had died of strangulation. All evidence of the affair was quickly swept away, the weight was raised and locked in place, the upper bucket was refilled to the proper mark and the lower bucket emptied, and the chamber was ready for the hanging of Peter Agusta.

At 9:00 p.m. Warden Cleghorn appeared at the cell door and read the death warrant and the long record of respites to Agusta. The prisoner's wrists and arms were bound and he was escorted the dozen steps into the death chamber. He also had declined to speak to the witnesses, so he stood in front of the platform while his knees and ankles were bound, the noose was positioned and cinched, and the black hood was pulled over his head from behind, and in that condition he was lifted onto the platform. All eyes again turned to the gauge on the wall, and at 9:15 p.m. the 300-pound weight fell and Agusta's body jerked into the air. This time the condemned man's neck was broken in the jerk, and in a few minutes Dr. Dawson, assisted by Dr. A. R. Richardson, pronounced the prisoner dead. While the body was being cut down and removed to the storage room, the witnesses retired to the warden's office to sign the death certificates. They had been invited to spend the night in prison quarters, so they remained within the prison's walls, avoiding the small crowd gathered at the gate.

The bodies of Jordan and Agusta were carried to the prison's operating room in their coffins, where an autopsy was conducted as required by law. Agusta had no one to take charge of his body, so he was returned to the plain pine coffin provided by the county. He received a pauper's funeral the following day when he was buried in the Catholic cemetery following a brief service. On the day of the execution, between the time of James Jordan's morning and evening visits, Thomas Jordan's brother made arrangements at Pauls & Penny, Undertakers, to take charge of the body of Thomas Jordan and prepare it for burial, then host a wake. The remains of Thomas A. Jordan were moved into a fine coffin and he was also buried in the Catholic cemetery the following day, but with a more elaborate service conducted by the priest and a small gathering of friends and family in attendance.

CHAPTER 10

A Train Robbery in Cow Creek Canyon

John "Jack" Case was only twenty-two years old when he first arrived at the Oregon State Penitentiary on February 2, 1886, and was registered as prisoner No. 1760. He had been convicted of "larceny in a store" and was sentenced to serve a term of five years, but he was released on January 9, 1889, after serving less than three years. There is no record of his criminal offenses during the next ten months, but on Saturday, November 9, 1889, Case was burglarizing a house when he was discovered by resident Charles Kallich, whom he knocked to the ground and cut his throat with a razor before fleeing. Kallich recovered and described his attacker. On Tuesday, November 12, Case, with sixty-year-old Myron D. Lockwood, alias Bassett, tried to rob a Chinese wood chopper's camp outside of Albina, Oregon, near Portland on the northern border of the state. Case had been posted at the door of their dwelling, and he was armed with one of Lockwood's pair of five-shot Bulldog revolvers to see that none escaped while Lockwood went in to gather their plunder. Case was distracted when he saw a Chinaman walking about outside the dwelling, and just then he heard gunshots fired. He fired his pistol but missed the Chinaman, and as he fled he felt a blow to his head. Ah Mine, the Chinese cook, had guessed what was happening and had snuck up behind Case and struck him in the head with a hatchet. The wound caused a deep gash at the hair line that ran back onto his scalp, but the consequent scar was later covered by hair carefully combed over.

Lockwood had been chopped horribly and died soon afterward, and his inquest was held on Thursday. One of the Chinamen inside the dwelling had also been seriously wounded, but he survived. Case rushed to Sister's Hospital in Vancouver, Washington, where he was arrested by the city marshal. Case confessed to the attempted robbery and later identified the two Bulldog revolvers, and he learned that Lockwood had fired all five shots. Case was extradited to Multnomah County and appeared before district court judge Loyal B. Stearns on November 25. He pled guilty, was sentenced to serve seven years in prison, and was registered as prisoner No. 2293. James W. Poole arrived at the penitentiary on June 20, 1890, sentenced to serve three years for a manslaughter committed in Douglas County, and he was registered as prisoner No. 2378. The two convicts became friends. On appeal Poole was granted a retrial, acquitted of the manslaughter charge but convicted of "obtaining money by false pretenses," and sentenced to serve another year. He returned, was registered as prisoner No. 2690 and was released on July 19, 1892. Case was released two years later on April 6, 1894. The two men rendezvoused, and they spent the next year planning a train robbery.

Cow Creek Canyon was a lonely place in 1895, thirty miles south of Roseburg and eight miles south of Riddles in Douglas County, Oregon. The mountain passes in the canyon were of such a peculiar formation, with many sharp curves, that trains had to travel at a slow rate of speed, never exceeding twenty-six miles an hour in the dry season and much slower in the wet season. On Monday evening, July 1, the canyon was pitch-black despite a bright moon because the moonlight was blocked by the precipitous mountain on one side of the canyon, which was covered with heavy timber that made it seem all the more dark and gloomy. At 10:15 p.m. the Southern Pacific's California Express northbound train No. 15 entered Cow Creek Canyon. The only light for the train was the powerful headlamp and, to the sides, the dim lights from inside the cars. Fireman Everett L. Gray was stoking the engine to get up a good head of steam before they reached the steep grade ahead, and he was being assisted by a hobo who had hitched a ride and agreed to work rather than be put off the train. Suddenly there was an explosion under the engine, and engineer J. B. Waite, thinking it was a warning torpedo set by a section crew making repairs ahead, immediately applied the brakes. This first explosion blew away the flanges of the pony trucks, disabling the engine, and as the train came to a halt there was an explosion to the front of the train and another in the rear, but neither of these explosions caused any damage to the train or tracks. As the train sat idling, and the trainmen were contemplating their next move, three masked men approached the train. The leader, at gunpoint, took the engineer, fireman, and the hobo prisoner out of the engine cab. R. E. Smith, an insurance salesman, along with two friends, stuck their heads out of the smoker window to see what was happening but retreated quickly when a robber pointed a gun at them. Conductor Kearney ran forward to determine the problem and nearly ran into one of the robbers, who fired a warning shot and ordered, "Get inside and stay there." Kearney went to the Pullman car and from there he could see one of the robbers patrolling the bank above the cars, so he hid.

The lead robber, the only one to make personal contact with the trainmen, took Waite, Gray, and the hobo to the Wells, Fargo express car and demanded that expressman Ralph M. Donohue open the doors. The expressman had had the presence of mind, at the first alarm, to remove the treasure from the local express box. He had hidden it under some goods and relocked the box, and when the order came to open the door he surrendered without resistance. All the hostages piled in and the robber ordered them to keep their hands up, and then told Donohue to open the safes, and the local box was unlocked. The robber found nothing he wanted and ordered the through-safe opened, but Donohue said he did not have the combination. The robber said, "I believe you are lying, but I'll come back and blow it up with dynamite." Then he drew a bead on Donohue's head and said, "I'll give you just five minutes to open that safe." The plucky expressman replied, "Well, you are simply wasting time. I can't and won't open it. The combination is not given me, just because of such occurrences as this. So if you are going to shoot if I don't open it, you are wasting time to wait five minutes." The robber replied, "You're hot stuff, ain't you!"

They remained in the express car a little more than ten minutes before the robbers took the four hostages to the mail car, which mail clerk C. A. Hermann opened only after being threatened with dynamiting of the car. The lead robber needed assistance getting into the mail car, and this was supplied by his hostages, and once inside his first demand was for the registered mail. Hermann later said he had little mail when they left the station at Glendale and when he discovered the train was being robbed he had spread the local packages and registered pouches about the coach in various hiding places, so when required he produced only three of the registered pouches and this seemed to be all he had. The robber made Hermann cut them open at the point of his pistol and then had him take out the packages and throw them on the floor at the robber's feet. The robber tore open the packages, taking out the money but throwing away all the other contents. He next asked for the local packages and Hermann replied, "It's Sunday, you know, and I haven't many. They are scattered in those pouches." The robber then went through the few pouches indicated and took out only five packages, leaving unmolested forty-five others that were well hidden. "What kind of ticker do you have?" the robber asked, and Hermann said, "I have an old one given me by my father some years ago." The robber told him to keep it and then ordered him to join the party. Hermann pleaded that he had not slept for many hours, and he looked very tired. He asked to be allowed to shut the door and sleep, and he was permitted to do so.

The robbers' leader then took the hostages to the first passenger car, which was a day coach. Donohue walked ahead with a lantern and was followed by the hobo, who was carrying an empty sack supplied by the robber. The party went through the coaches from front to back, first the two day coaches, then two tourist sleepers, a smoker, and two Pullman sleepers. As they proceeded through the train, the party picked up the two brakemen and the porter, named "Old Squab," making eight hostages in all, but they left J. G. Ryan, the colored buffet man, at his station. In each car the robber announced, "Remain perfectly quiet, gentlemen. If I am hurt, you'll all go too. I have a dozen men outside loaded down with dynamite, and you'd better not try to be funny." Sometimes he also remarked, "I'll give you a lift if any harm comes to me." To emphasize their resolve, robbers walked along each side of the train at the same pace as the interior party, firing their pistols into the air periodically and exploding a stick of dynamite every few minutes. At each seat in the forward passenger cars, the plunder was gathered by Old Squab and put into the sack carried by the hobo. In the smoker they encountered a man about twenty-three years old who began to cry when told to "dig." "What's the matter?" the robber asked, feigning sympathy, and he replied, "That's all the money I've got," as he handed over a few dollars. "Is that so?" replied the robber with a simulated whimper. "That's too bad," he added and then pretended to burst into tears. Still, he had Old Squab take the money and put it in the sack. When he came to Klamath County Sheriff A. A. Fitch, who was transporting a prisoner, the lawman said he had no money, only a revolver, and the robber took his blue steel B caliber Colt revolver with black handles. When the party reached the sleeper cars, the robber asked at each berth, "Man or lady?" and Old Squab would tell him. He robbed only the men who were in the lower berths and took nothing from the women or from any man who appeared to be a laborer.

He asked one man, "Got any money?" The man replied, "A little," and the robber said, "Well, keep it. You look like a hard-working man and I guess you need it." He told a pair of passengers, "Oh, you're broke, I suppose? And you too, poor fellow. Dig up. Got a watch? Let's see it." When the second man produced an old watch, the robber said he could not use it in his business and threw it on the floor. He seemed somewhat disgusted at the poverty of the passengers, whom he described as "silver men." Describing himself as a "gold bug," the robber told them to dig for their gold, but most of the passengers had suspected what was happening before his arrival and had hidden their valuables before he appeared. The process of going through the coaches took more than fifteen minutes, and near the end of the ordeal the robber seemed anxious. On several occasions he asked his hostages to tell him the time. Once the party of hostages and the robber-leader stepped onto the rear platform of the last car, the trainmen were ordered to the front of the train.

Old Squab, who had been left on the platform, called to the robber, "Let me know when you're through, sir, and I'll tell the conductor." The robber replied, laughing, "Get in that car, you black rascal, or I'll blow your head off. I'll let you know in plenty of time to start the train." Seeing that the robbing was done and the robber was in a good mood, the engineer expressed concern for his engine. He said he wanted to check it, but the robber said, "Oh, damn your engine! You stay where you are." As the rest of the party moved forward, the expressman and fireman were directed into the express car. They were ordered to close the door, and then the engineer was allowed to go to his engine. Once inside the express car, Donohue gave a shotgun he had hidden to fireman Gray, and he grabbed his revolver to await the return of the robber, who had promised earlier to come back and blow up the through-safe. However, when the hostage party got to the engine, the robber-leader just continued walking until he came upon his two partners. He then turned and fired three shots, putting out the engine's headlamp. The three men walked into the brush and disappeared into the darkness. By the time Donohue and Gray got the door of the express car opened, they were unable to get a clean shot at the robbers, who kept shooting until they were entirely out of sight. Their take was soon calculated at about $1,000 from the mails and $520.70 from the passengers, but nothing had been taken from the express car. The damage to the train required the engine to be uncoupled and taken to a siding where it could be turned around. The engine was then used to drive the train into Roseburg backwards, which delayed the report of the robbery another three hours.

Superintendent Fields of the Southern Pacific Railroad telegraphed Sheriff Joseph G. Hiatt of Josephine County to go in pursuit of the robbers and to spare neither effort nor expense. The following day a "wanted" circular was issued by Oregon's line manager, R. Koehler, in which he described the inside man as "5 foot 11 inches in height, native born American . . . light complexion, light moustache, hair cut close, light gray or blue eyes . . . weight about 170, high cheek bones, upper jaw protrudes over the lower one, bridge of nose swollen as though poisoned with poison oak, [wearing] blue overalls with jumper, light checkered vest or checkered cotton shirt, heavy stodgy shoes about number 8. The Southern Pacific Company will pay a reward of two thousand dollars ($2000) for the arrest and conviction of each of the robbers." It was also noted by some witnesses that the leader of the robber gang seemed to be familiar with trains, was about thirty years old, and had a rich baritone voice. Koehler later amended his reward offer to say that it was being jointly offered by the railroad and Wells, Fargo & Company, and it included the standing reward per robber offered by Wells, Fargo.

In response to the robbery and the rewards, several posses were formed. Some were on their way to the scene while others spread into the countryside trying to intercept the robbers on their most likely routes of escape. Douglas County Sheriff C. F. Cathcart and Riddles's constable George Quine rushed to the scene of the robbery with a small posse. Quine was an amateur detective, so when he found evidence he documented it carefully. There was a campfire near the tracks where the robbers had apparently waited for some time for the train's arrival, and there Quine found distinctive boot prints, one with two rows of tacks in the heels. The foot tracks were followed to the place where the robbers mounted, and the posse then followed the trail of horse tracks. One of the horse's shoes had quite a peculiar design, and the trail led them to a more permanent camp, where they matched the horse tracks and boot prints. They also found the masks, which had been made from sugar sacks, and a rag from a flour sack used to bind a wound. They learned that the robbers had used giant powder sticks three-quarters of an inch in diameter, which were not used by the railroad but by miners. It was believed the men had brought them some distance to do the work and were probably miners or acquainted with mining.

On July 2 Stilly Riddle, who lived near the town of Riddles, went into Roseburg after he heard all the details of the train robbery, especially the description of the men. He reported that there were three men who had been working for some time at Nichols station, which was thirteen miles south of Riddles, and at least the lead robber matched the description of one of those men. Two of the men had been seen near the site of the robbery the day before it happened. They were heading toward the tracks, but after the robbery they seemed to disappear from the area. One, according to Riddle, always wore a white hat with a buckskin band, just like the one described as worn by the robber who went through the train cars. He said he knew the men as John Case and James Poole. It happened that the lawmen were familiar with these two men, who had met after being sent to prison in 1890 on separate charges. Poole had been released in 1892 and Case two years later, and they settled near Canyonville, living off and on with Poole's father, Napoleon. With the focus now on named suspects, the search centered on Napoleon Poole's house, where his sons Jim and Albert were arrested within a few days. Napoleon also let the lawmen search his house, where they found sacking and string that matched that in the robber's camp, and both Jim and Albert Poole's boots matched exactly the boot prints with the peculiar double-tack design on the heels. Case was arrested later that day. He would be identified as the man who had gone through the coaches, as his mask of light cloth had revealed his face to many of his victims.

At their preliminary hearing the three men were held to answer to the US grand jury. They were indicted and taken to Portland, where they were lodged in jail to await trial at the fall session. Though they were questioned closely, they would not confess nor "peach," or inform, on one another. The trial of the Poole brothers and Case began in the US district court in mid-December on a charge of robbing the US mail. The trial lasted five days, one to seat the jury and four days to take testimony. On Christmas eve at 3:00 p.m., after one hour of deliberations, the jury returned a verdict of guilty for Jim Poole and John Case but not guilty for Albert Poole, and the third robber was never identified. Everyone on the defense side of the case was astonished with the verdict against Jim Poole because the evidence against him was no stronger than the evidence against his brother. Even Judge Charles B. Bellinger said, "I am frank to say that I am not entirely satisfied with the verdict." Still, when defense attorneys W. W. Cardwell and Albert Abraham filed a motion for a new trial, it was denied by Judge Bellinger. The prisoners were remanded to the custody of the sheriff and returned to their jail cells while the attorneys filed an appeal with the California Supreme Court.

Poole and Case were never taken to the prison but remained in Portland until the decision of the lower court was overturned in June 1896. The following month the prisoners were released on their own recognizance. Case began working his way up the coast toward Tacoma,

John Case
SAN FRANCISCO CHRONICLE: JANUARY 30, 1897

James Poole
SAN FRANCISCO CHRONICLE: JANUARY 30, 1897

Washington, probably committing petty crimes along the way, and he was conspicuous in several cities because of his rowdy behavior. On January 28, 1897, a train was robbed at Shady Point, Oregon, two miles west of Roseburg. Case was suspected, but there was no evidence to implicate him, so he was not arrested. Case finally reached Tacoma in May 1897 and began planning a robbery. On May 23 he tried to rob the Stellacoom streetcar but Superintendent Frank Dame was aboard. Dame drew his pistol and exchanged shots with Case. Although shot in the left arm, Dame managed to mortally wound Case. At the robber's inquest Case was positively identified by three men who knew him; his picture had arrived from Roseburg and perfected the identification. In September 1897, with Case dead, the indictments against Poole and Case were dismissed, so no one ever served time in prison for the Cow Creek Canyon train robbery.

CHAPTER 11

Jerked to Jesus!

William Wallace "Billy" Calder, his younger brother "Jimmy," and James Eli "Dee" Fisher lived on a ranch a few miles from the Musselshell River in southeastern Fergus County, Montana. In Billings, Lewistown, and other area settlements, the three men had built a reputation as petty crooks, with Billy considered their leader. On September 24, 1898, the three men went to the sheep ranch of Farquhar McRae, which was situated a few miles from their ranch, intending to murder him and steal his flock of 1,700 sheep. The plan was to have Billy engage McRae in friendly conversation, and, while thus preoccupied, Fisher was to shoot him in the head. When they arrived, McRae was herding a portion of his flock, and Billy, as agreed, distracted him in conversation by speaking of the fine condition of his sheep and congratulating him on his prospects. However, Fisher seemed immobilized as Billy signaled to him several times to shoot McRae. When Fisher failed to move, Billy, swearing an oath, snatched the rifle from his hands, put it to McRae's head, and fired, killing the sheepman instantly. Once McRae fell, Billy kicked the body and said, "'Tis no more than killing the dogs to kill him." They stripped the dead man of all his valuables and tied a rope to the body and dragged it to McRae's cabin.

Fisher, embarrassed by his inability to act, announced that he would kill McRae's herder, John Allen, so that they could get the rest of the sheep. He left but returned shortly, saying, "She's off," meaning he had killed the sheepherder. The three men then dragged Allen's body to the cabin. There they wrapped McRae's body in a quilt, wrapped Allen's body in a tarpaulin, and then cached both bodies in an old chimney on the ranch. They spent the night in McRae's cabin, which gave them ample time to carefully ransack the home for any valuables that might be hidden there. The next morning they hitched up McRae's team to his wagon, placed both bodies beneath a load of bacon, ham, flour, dried and canned fruit, and all their plunder, and they drove toward Forsyth in Custer County. They herded the sheep with them. Along the way they asked everyone they met if they had seen McRae, explaining that the sheepherder had sold them his flock and had promised to help them load the sheep at Forsyth, and they were confident that this ruse would serve as their alibi. When the murderers reached the Musselshell, they camped beside the river and built a big fire of drift wood. They removed the bodies from the wagon, cut them into pieces, and threw the body parts into the fire, which was kept roaring until nothing but calcined bones, belt buckles, and metal rivets from the victims' clothing remained. These they threw in the river before proceeding on to Forsyth.

News of McRae's disappearance did not reach Lewistown until a week after the murders. The Calders and Fisher were immediately suspected, so a posse started out and caught the three fugitives at Forsyth. The ashes of the suspiciously large fire were discovered and the river was dragged, and the bones and belt buckles were recovered. Once the murderers were lodged in jail, Jimmy, the weakest of the three, was promised that he would be punished by imprisonment for a term of only two years if he would tell the truth, so he confessed to every detail. The Calder boys' mother, Mrs. Sam Smith, also gave testimony against Billy to save Jimmy. On March 25, 1899, Billy Calder was convicted of murder in the first degree. Six days later Fisher was also convicted. Both defendants were sentenced to hang on May 12, 1899, and both men had their attorneys file an appeal. Fisher was granted a new trial, which was to be held at Fort Benton in July, but the state supreme court denied Billy's appeal.

On March 10, 1900, Judge Dudley DuBose brought Billy into court and asked him if he had any reason why sentence should not be imposed upon him. Billy responded with a lengthy harangue citing every possible reason he could think of, all of which had been considered and disposed of by the supreme court. Judge DuBose then said that he had sentenced too many men to hang, and that a long wait for an execution was not a kindness. He said, ". . . I believe that the shorter the time is, the better it is for him and the better for the state. Viewing it in that light—a kindness to you—I have made the time very short." The judge then proceeded to sentence Billy to hang on Friday, March 16, 1900, only one week from that date, between the hours of 9:00 a.m. and 5:00 p.m.

After the convictions of his brother and Fisher, Jimmy Calder recanted his testimony. Billy, it was clear, was lost, but by changing his testimony Jimmy believed he could still save Fisher. He claimed now that he and Fisher had been some distance from the ranch in a coulee when the killings occurred, and they had not taken part in the butchery at the river. He claimed that Billy alone had killed both men and disposed of the bodies. As a consequence of reneging on his plea deal, Jimmy was scheduled to be tried on a charge of first-degree murder. Fisher's second trial began on April 24, 1900, but the jury deadlocked eleven for acquittal and one for conviction and death. After four hours of deliberation, they compromised and acquitted Fisher. Jimmy Calder was tried next, but the charge of murder was dropped. Instead he was tried for perjury based upon the circumstance that he had testified under oath to two completely conflicting stories, and one had to be perjury. Billy was convicted and sentenced to serve six years at the state prison in Deer Lodge. He served his time as a model prisoner and was released on July 30, 1904.

The execution of Billy Calder was the first legal execution in Fergus County. The gallows had been assembled in advance and was of the twitch-up design. A twitch-up gallows drops a great weight attached to the end of the hangman's rope opposite the noose; in this case the weight was a large box that could hold anything with an aggregate weight sufficient to jerk the condemned man off a low platform. Sheriff Thomas Shaw selected scrap iron, which was readily available, and he had batches weighed until the accumulated weight was 308 pounds. The gallows had been constructed to accommodate two men, in the belief that Fisher would hang with Billy, but now the second pulley, through which the hangman's rope would have been threaded, dangled unused. Sheriff Shaw had not witnessed a hanging previously and wanted to take no chances, so he had the dirt excavated a foot deep under the platform, and a rope was tied to one corner of the platform. If, after the condemned was jerked up, the stretching of the rope or the stretch to Billy's neck left his toes touching the platform, it could be pulled out to allow an additional foot of clearance. The excavation of the dirt led some to later conclude that Billy Calder had been dropped into a deep hole and buried on the spot.

During the last few days of his life, Billy mellowed and finally accepted the religious teachings of Presbyterian Reverend Albert Pfaus, expressing a belief in God but avoiding any discussion of the possibility of a future existence. On Wednesday, March 14, Billy asked for a meeting with his brother Jimmy. Billy severely criticized him for lying about Fisher's part in the killing of Allen, but Jimmy stood firm and the meeting ended without resolution. Billy's mother visited her son at 9:30 on the morning of his execution. As she left, his last words to her were, "I forgive you for all you ever did. Good-bye." Billy, when he could think of no one else to blame, had blamed his mother for his upbringing, which he implied had led to his execution.

Father James A. Vermaat joined the prisoner and Reverend Pfaus in the cell after Calder's mother left. The priest offered to hear the condemned man's final confession, but he declined. When Sheriff Shaw began reading the death warrant, Billy interrupted and asked him to hurry, as he was concerned he might lose his nerve. After the reading the straps were brought out and each wrist was secured to a thigh, then a large strap about his chest bound his arms at the elbows. As soon as he was bound, the sheriff left for the gallows, as it was his duty to release the weight, and he took his position behind a curtain on the right side of the scaffolding. The prisoner walked to the gallows with Undersheriff Lincoln P. Slater guiding him by the arm, and they arrived at 10:35 a.m. The prisoner nodded to several men he recognized among the witnesses, but he made no remarks of significance. This was a surprise, as the condemned man was expected to make a detailed confession but again refused to do so. Outside the twelve-foot wooden fence surrounding the jail yard, three hundred spectators had assembled, but they could see nothing of the execution.

Billy took his place under the noose, then turned to face the crowd and complained, "The sun is shining in my eyes." Slater quickly pinioned Billy's legs at the knees and ankles with straps, the noose was positioned and cinched to hold it in place, and a black bag was readied. Billy was then given the opportunity to address the witnesses, and the condemned man slowly looked over the seventy spectators, which included lawmen, the attending physicians, and newspaper reporters, before he said, "Well, boys, I bid you all good-bye. I have told Mr. Johns all I could tell. All I can say now is that I am innocent." The black bag was pulled over his head and the drawstrings tightened, and in but a moment, at 10:41 a.m., the cord supporting the weighted box was cut. The great weight dropped, jerking the condemned man skyward two feet and breaking his neck. The body rebounded and came to rest with Billy's toes four inches above the wooden platform, so it was not pulled away. The body convulsed almost immediately, and then after a few minutes it twitched several more times before becoming motionless. Doctor H. H. Wilson, who had been standing close and watching the

Billy Calder is prepared by Undersheriff Lincoln P. Slater with Dr. H. H. Wilson looking on.

preparations, waited three minutes before stepping forward to search for a pulse, and he found a strong heartbeat. He conferred with two other attending physicians who were there to witness the activities, and then he checked the pulse every few minutes until, after ten minutes, the pulse was beginning to weaken. During the next four minutes, the body visibly relaxed, and Billy finally unclenched his fists. When his heart ceased to beat at 10:55 a.m., Dr. Wilson pronounced him dead. After hanging five minutes more, the body was cut down and lowered into a coffin, which had been stored around the corner of the jail and brought forward. The noose and hood were removed and the lid closed. Six men carried the coffin to a hearse waiting outside the jail yard, where Billy's mother waited to take charge of her son's remains. The hearse was driven to Hobensack & Stoddard's Funeral Parlor and prepared for burial. The following morning William Wallace Calder was laid to rest in the little cemetery just west of Lewistown.

CHAPTER 12

They Killed the Captain

Oliver Dotson earned his nickname "the Captain" during his youth as the commander of a Mississippi riverboat. Later he drifted to South Dakota, where he lived for many years and, though an eccentric, married and raised a large family. At age sixty-seven he moved to American Gulch, fifteen miles north of Avon, Montana, and three miles west of Washington Gulch along the Northern Pacific rail line. Both gulches had been prosperous placer mining camps a quarter of a century earlier, but now only old-timers who had hung on when the gold played out lived there. Captain Dotson and his son-in-law, Edward Cachelin, mined the placers and did well enough to fill their cupboard with food and have a few dollars left. In 1899 Captain Dotson's son Clinton and his grandson Oliver Benson came from South Dakota for a visit. They stayed several weeks and then started for Helena with a span of small horses and a wagon. A few days after they left, Eugene Cullinane, a close neighbor of Captain Dotson, was found murdered. Dotson's son and grandson were suspected. Two days after the grisly discovery, the two suspected murderers and a third man named Ellis Persinger were arrested near Bozeman, Montana, still driving the same team and wagon. In the bedtick of the wagon was found Cullinane's watch, and all three were charged with Cullinane's murder. The watch proved to be the strongest evidence against them, as they could not explain how they had possession of the watch if they were not guilty of murder.

They were convicted, but Benson and Persinger received only ten-year prison terms while Clinton Dotson was sentenced to serve a life term.

At the prison Clinton Dotson shared a cell with James McArthur, who was about to be released. McArthur (sometimes spelled MacArthur), alias James Fleming, was a career criminal when he was sentenced to serve a term at the Deer Lodge prison. Dotson fooled McArthur into believing that he had cached $15,000 from a train robbery in Wyoming, and he promised to pay McArthur half that sum if he would perform a task for him. McArthur appreciated the ingenuity of Dotson's plan, and the payoff, so he agreed to help his cell mate get a pardon. Dotson then told Persinger and Benson about his plan to gain a pardon for all three convicted men: He would have McArthur forge a will and confession allegedly signed by Captain Dotson that would clear Clinton of Cullinane's murder, reveal that the Captain had killed his neighbor, and implicate Cachelin as the man who had planted Cullinane's watch in the bedtick of their wagon. McArthur would then kill the Captain so he could not refute the documents. Persinger went to the warden and told him the details of the plan, but it seemed so bizarre and unprecedented in the annals of crime that he was not believed.

As soon as McArthur was released, he traveled to Washington Gulch, where Captain Dotson had moved after his son was convicted of the murder in American Gulch. McArthur carried an introduction from the Captain's son, and he befriended the old man. He stayed with the Captain, which gave him an opportunity to study his host's handwriting, and he traveled with the Captain to various places during the next few weeks. On January 10 the Captain contracted smallpox and was sent to the pesthouse in Helena, where he remained until mid-February. McArthur returned to the Captain's cabin and used this unexpected opportunity to make his preparations. The interior of the cabin was divided into two rooms by a plank partition; McArthur cut a square hole in one plank about five feet above the floor, and he covered it with a cloth so that the back room remained darkened. On the morning of February 1, McArthur went to the cabin of Herman Ruther and borrowed a bottle of ink, which he returned that evening. Captain Dotson returned home from the pesthouse on the morning of February 15, 1901, and a few minutes after he entered his cabin a shot was heard by several neighbors. At 2:00 p.m. McArthur was seen leaving the Captain's cabin heading southward toward Avon, and he was seen again passing the home of Michael Killey a mile south; yet a mile farther he passed two men who knew him. He reached Avon, where a half dozen men recognized him, at 6:00 p.m. On February 16 McArthur sent a coded letter to the penitentiary stating that the work was done.

On February 19 the body of Captain Dotson was found shot through the head and lying in the east part of the front room. On a washstand were two handwritten documents, one a will and the other a confession, and the body and circumstances were made to look like a suicide. A gun was fastened to the wall pointing in the direction of the body, a string attached to the trigger passed backwards around a nail, and the end of the string had been dropped between the Captain's feet. One shell in the gun was empty. However, a careful examination of the scene revealed that the body had not fallen at that spot, and a large pool of blood was found poorly concealed in the northeast corner of the room. A trail of blood ran from the pool of blood to where the body was found, showing it had been moved after death, and the hair on the back of the Captain's head was turned backward, indicating he had been dragged by his feet. The documents on the washstand were not in the Captain's handwriting, and experts would later testify that these two documents had been written with McArthur's hand and were badly disguised to appear as if the Captain had written them. The will left everything to Clinton Dotson while the confession said that the Captain and his son-in-law, Ed Cachelin, had murdered Eugene

James McArthur murders Captain Dotson.
BUTTE MINER: APRIL 5, 1902

Cullinane. The confession explained that at the Captain's insistence Cachelin took Cullinane's watch to Helena and hid it in the bedtick of Clinton Dotson's wagon, which had resulted in the conviction of three innocent men. The document said that guilt and remorse had driven the Captain to commit suicide.

McArthur was immediately suspected, and a search for him began. Although he was well schooled in the tramp's method of traveling unseen on trains and therefore could have easily avoided capture, he had developed a fondness for the daughter of a Missoula County rancher, a Mr. Berry. He lingered at the ranch courting the girl and was quickly apprehended. McArthur, when arrested, talked freely of the details of the crime and Clinton Dotson's part in planning it. James McArthur and Clinton Dotson were charged with the murder of Captain Dotson, but they were tried separately, McArthur first. McArthur was convicted of first-degree murder, and Judge J. M. Clements of Helena sentenced him to hang on September 16, 1901. Dotson was then tried and also convicted of first-degree murder. Judge Clements sentenced Dotson to hang with McArthur, but Dotson obtained a respite while the state supreme court considered the conviction and sentence of the lower court. After the conviction and sentence were affirmed, Dotson was sentenced to hang on April 4, 1902.

Nothing intervened to delay McArthur's execution so, as September 16 approached, a sixteen-foot-tall rough-board fence was erected in the southeast corner of the jail yard enclosing an area of five thousand square feet. The scaffold was the same on which convicted murderer Daniel Lucey had been hanged on September 14, 1900, and it was thoroughly tested. In the northeast corner of the enclosure, diagonally in front of the gallows, a stand had been erected for the press. McArthur was watched closely because he had vowed after his conviction that he would cheat the hangman. Two weeks prior to his date with the executioner, he used a needle, the only implement he could obtain, to sever several arteries in his wrist and thumb, but once weakened from the loss of blood he called for help. He was saved by the doctors and bedridden for two days recovering. He constantly pleaded with visitors to bring poison and made other feeble attempts at self-destruction, so at times he was double-ironed, or chained at the wrist and ankle. On the morning before his execution, he was visited by Fathers Phelan of Helena and Aikens of Philipsburg. Through their counseling he seemed to become resigned to his fate, and by midday Thursday McArthur was "as jovial as a man at a fair" when he greeted a newspaper reporter. The morning newspaper had said McArthur treated death as a joke, and he responded, "Could I regard death as a joke, could any man? It is a serious thing; I am going to meet my Maker because people want me to. I am innocent of the crime for which my life must pay the penalty. But, who cares?" He said that his friends would clear his name and that his brothers Will from Butte and John from Lisbon, South Dakota, were now in town. Later he confided to the sheriff and undersheriff that he had a wife and two daughters in South Dakota, saying, "They never wanted for anything when I had anything to give them. Why, once I held a man up in Helena and took $400 from him and expressed every cent of it to my family, going broke myself."

On McArthur's final night he was watched by Charles Aspling and Frank Comstock. He could not sleep, so he stayed up all night talking with the two deputies, who had been locked in his cell to prevent him from committing suicide. Several times he called for whiskey, and the liquor braced him up. A *Butte Inter Mountain* newspaper reporter called at 2:00 a.m., and McArthur warned, "Don't sleep too late, you must be here on time to see me jerked." At daybreak the prisoner yelled to the jailor, "Come on, McMahon, I was to be up early for breakfast. He said five o'clock. Come on there and get breakfast for me, you fellows have got to hang me at ten o'clock." However, breakfast was delayed until after McArthur received Holy Communion from Father Phelan, who was accompanied by two Sisters of Charity, at 8:00 a.m. The prisoner was baptized into the Catholic faith, and this was followed by a mass. Then the priest, after hearing McArthur's confession, administered last rites. Once the priest and nuns left the jail, the prisoner grew moody. While being shaved, he began complaining about every inconsequential matter.

McArthur ate breakfast at 8:30 a.m., and then his brothers were admitted. While visiting, the condemned man was dressed in his burial clothes, a neat fitting black suit with turned-down collar and a black bow tie. He continued to protest his innocence, but he now accused the Captain's neighbor Perry Ouchley and Ed Cachelin of killing the Captain. As the fatal moment approached, McArthur was visited by Fathers Phelan and Aikens, who brought along Father Thompson, and they prayed with him. At 10:08 a.m. Sheriff John McMahon read the death warrant, and this seemed to settle the prisoner. The procession to the gallows began at 10:15 a.m. with Fathers Phelan and Thompson leading, Father Aikens on the prisoner's right and Sheriff McMahon on his left, and Undersheriff Dee and his two deathwatch guards taking up the rear. As they passed Clinton Dotson's cell, McArthur's accomplice asked, "Won't you forgive me, Mac?" McArthur replied, "I can say good-bye but I can't forgive." But then at the strong urging of one of the priests, he forgave the man who had placed him in this predicament. Dotson then collapsed and cried like a small child.

A winter storm had blown through town from 9:00 p.m. the previous night until 4:00 a.m. The snow had melted, so now it was cold and wet in the jail yard, and it was still heavily overcast. As McArthur stepped into the yard, he hesitated for a moment to examine the machine of execution and then glanced at the crowd of one hundred fifty witnesses. He walked to the platform and took his place beneath the noose. "Friends," he called out, "I want your attention for a few moments. I am about to meet my Maker. I am here to die an innocent man. I have been wronged and God knows it. I forgive everybody. I go with a clear conscience to meet my Maker. I thank you for your attention and am now ready to meet my Maker. Good-bye, all!" The sheriff waited until he was done speaking and then pinioned his arms and legs, and McArthur assisted in adjusting the noose and black hood by tilting his head. When all was prepared at 10:20 a.m., the restraining rope was cut and the 312-pound weight dropped. McArthur was jerked into the air and the condemned man's neck was neatly broken, so that the body displayed neither a convulsion nor a twitch. After fifteen minutes county physician Dr. J. H. Owens, assisted by Drs. Glass and E. F. Dodds, could feel no pulse, so at 10:43 a.m. they pronounced the prisoner dead. McArthur's remains were lowered into a casket and turned over to undertaker M. Bien for preparation. One hour later the body of James McArthur was interred in a plot provided by prison Warden Frank Conley.

Dotson continued to await word on his appeal. When it was eventually denied, the application for a commutation of sentence was submitted to Governor Joseph K. Toole. Following denial of the appeal, there immediately followed a deluge of letters to the governor requesting the commutation of Dotson's sentence, including a letter from a mother of nine children claiming to be Clinton Dotson's wife. That letter was accompanied by a heartbreaking letter from her twelve-year-old daughter. For days before his execution date, Dotson expressed a horror of the crowd, saying, "I don't mind to die, but I do hate to face the crowd that will be here to see me go through this awful ordeal. If it was not for that I wouldn't care." On the day before his execution, Dotson slept until ten o'clock and awoke with a surly attitude. Reverend A. B. Martin arrived to provide spiritual comfort and sat with him while he ate a hearty breakfast. Sheriff McMahon had ordered the suit of clothes Dotson would wear on the scaffold, and J. E. Maple of Butte arrived to take the prisoner's measurements. During the remainder of the morning and early afternoon, Dotson continued to hope for clemency, but word came at four o'clock that Governor Toole had refused to intervene. Dotson would not talk until he heard from the governor, but then he said, "I will give it up. I have fought this thing off as long as I can, and until I am tired and weak."

During his last evening Dotson ate a hearty supper and drank whiskey until, slightly intoxicated, he started chatting freely with reporters. He told a bit of his history, smoked several cigars, and stroked his graying beard as he talked. When asked about his part in his father's murder, he said, "I am ready to die but I am innocent of my father's death. I go hoping that people who have had it in for me will think of me kindly as they can. But I am innocent. That is all." That night Undersheriff Dee and Deputy Charles Aspling were locked in his cell to ensure that he did not take his own life. The whiskey he had been given did not sit well, and he became ill, but he finally fell asleep at 4:00 a.m. The prisoner was awake at 6:00 a.m., and an hour later the Sisters of Charity arrived to pray with him. When his breakfast was brought, his stomach was still queasy, but he managed to drink a little coffee. Father Phelan arrived at 10:50 a.m., and they were soon joined by Reverend Martin. The clergy provided support when Sheriff McMahon arrived at 11:20 a.m. to read the death warrant. As soon as the reading concluded, Dotson called for more whiskey and drank just enough to brace himself, and then the procession formed and the march to the gallows began.

Five hundred people surrounded the scaffold on April 4, 1902, when Dotson took his place on the platform, the same on which Lucey and McArthur had expiated their crimes. Dotson was asked if he had anything to say but he declined. At 11:26 a.m. the straps were applied to his wrists and arms, knees and ankles, and the noose was adjusted and cinched in place. It took only two minutes from the time the condemned man stepped onto the gallows to the moment when the black hood was pulled over his head, and the signal was immediately given to cut the restraining rope. The 312-pound weight dropped and Dotson's body shot upward, breaking his neck in the jerk. Doctors J. H. Owens and E. F. Dodds monitored Dotson's heart beat and pronounced him dead at 11:43 a.m. Dotson's remains were then lowered onto the platform and turned over to M. Bein & Son, Undertakers. That evening he was buried next to coconspirator James McArthur in a plot provided by prison Warden Conley.

CHAPTER 13

Murder on the High Seas

As the American West was settled it was supplied from the East Coast with all sorts of goods, including firearms, farm machinery, printing presses, and fine wines and liquors imported from Europe. At first most of these goods were brought west by ships traveling around Cape Horn and in freight wagon trains; later they were delivered partway by the railroads. After the transcontinental railroad was completed in 1869, goods were transported by train all the way to the Pacific coast. The West, in turn, supplied the East with cattle and sheep, animal pelts, buffalo robes and bones, artifacts of the western Indian tribes, and imports such as Philippine mahogany and spices and silk from Japan and China. Ships sailed west from San Diego and San Pedro, California, from Portland, Oregon, and from the Seattle, Washington, area. One of these ships, a schooner named the *Fred J. Wood*, sailed from Portland in mid-1902.

In early 1902 when Tanabara "Tom" Gisaburo was seventeen years old, he shipped out of Yokohama, Japan, bound for Portland, Oregon. Upon his arrival in Portland, he signed on as cabin boy aboard the *Fred J. Wood*, captained by Jorgen J. Jacobsen and registered out of Astoria, Oregon. The *Fred J. Wood* had been built for the E. K. Wood Lumber Company in 1899 by G. H. Hitchings at Hoquiam, Washington. It was a 681-ton, four-masted schooner with an eight-hundred-meter capacity. Besides the crew, Jacobsen had aboard his wife, Nettie,

Murderer Tanabara "Tom" Gisaburo
GABBIE HIRSCH

and their two children. The schooner, fully loaded with goods for trade in the Orient, left Astoria on July 20 bound for several Chinese ports, with its final destination at Hakodate, Japan. Gisaburo, a novice seaman who reportedly had been insubordinate toward the captain, believed that the captain was treating him badly and made up his mind to have revenge. On the evening of July 30, unbeknownst to cook Ohto, Gisaburo stole a large bread knife from the galley. On the morning of July 31, when the *Fred J. Wood* was six days east of Honolulu, Captain Jacobsen went below to awaken the cabin boy, who had failed to report for duty. As he was yanked out of bed, Gisaburo saw this as his chance. Without warning or hesitation, he drove the razor-sharp long-bladed bread knife into Jacobsen's groin, severing a major artery. The captain bled to death in seconds and fell on top of Gisaburo, pinning him to the floor. Mrs. Jacobsen had arisen at 6:50 a.m., and moments later she was notified that her husband had died. She hurried to the cabin and saw him lying on the floor. Thinking that a small dose of whiskey might revive him, she rushed to her cabin and hurriedly returned. She then saw, for the first time, the cabin boy lying beneath her husband's body, but she thought he was trying to help the captain rise. Jacobsen's body was lifted off Gisaburo, and the cabin boy, still holding the bloody knife, was overpowered and disarmed. The body of Jacobsen was taken onto the deck and examined in the sunlight, and then the cause of Captain Jacobsen's death became clear.

Mrs. Jacobsen cried out, "Tom, Tom. Why did you do this?" and he replied, "Captain hurt me!" Mrs. Jacobsen responded, "The captain never hurt you, but I feel like hurting you; as if I could kill you." Gisaburo replied, "I suppose you kill me now." Mrs. Jacobsen would later testify that she had, on a number of occasions, instructed Gisaburo in his duties and he seemed appreciative, causing her to believe he wanted to learn. Although Gisaburo apparently resented the captain's instructions, Mrs. Jacobsen testified that she had never seen the cabin boy being insubordinate. Gisaburo and cook Ohto, who slept near the cabin boy, were covered in blood, leading witnesses to believe Ohto was an accessory before the fact, so they were both locked in the hold still wearing their blood-soaked clothing. First Mate Henry Meyer, then in command, convened a court and tried the two men. Gisaburo, when allowed to testify, exonerated Ohto. Gisaburo was found guilty of murder and sentenced to hang. But the crew, upon the urging of Mrs. Jacobsen, decided to put into port at Honolulu and turn over their prisoner to the federal authorities, as murder on the high seas was a federal offense. Gisaburo remained locked away in the ship's hold still wearing his bloody clothing, while Ohto returned to his duties. The ship's carpenter prepared an airtight box made of heavy planks with the seams caulked. Jacobsen's body was washed and covered with alum, tightly wrapped in two sheets, and placed in the box. The box was filled with alcohol and covered with oakum before it was muffled up tightly by wrapping it in canvas sails, and then the coffin was tied down on the lumber stacked on the foredeck. This impromptu embalming left the body in perfect condition. When the ship reached Honolulu on August 5, the body looked natural, though "strong men winced as they saw the ghastly wound which had been inflicted by the Jap." Mrs. Jacobsen and her children, the crew on watch at the time of the murder, and cook Ohto were left in Honolulu while First Mate Meyer sailed on with the ship. The *Fred J. Wood* sailed to Portland and then returned to Astoria on December 12.

Ohto was again charged as an accessory, but he was released when it was clear that there was not enough evidence to hold him, especially because in each of Gisaburo's conflicting and confusing confessions he cleared the cook of any involvement. Gisaburo was retried in the federal court at Honolulu in late October and found guilty of first-degree murder. On October 31, 1902, he was sentenced by Judge Morris Estee to hang on December 26 and was delivered to the territorial prison at Oahu. Then, on Christmas day, Governor Sanford B. Dole telegraphed a reprieve, and President Theodore Roosevelt extended that reprieve to noon on August 14, 1903. All avenues of judicial and executive relief were finally exhausted when, on July 7, the president refused to interfere further. On July 18 Judge Estee ordered that the execution proceed on August 14 after noon, the date and time when the president's reprieve had run its course. When told of the order, Gisaburo said, "Huh! Too much scare! August 14, twelve o'clock go hang up rope." On Christmas Eve, 1902, as the time of his first execution date drew near, Gisaburo, who had been a Christian for four years, was reconverted and baptized by Reverend Motokawa of the Japanese Christian Church. Over the next eight months, the reverend attended to Gisaburo's religious needs, and finally he resigned himself to his fate. During his months in a prison cell, the prisoner had lost most of his appetite, but during his final hours he was served dainties prepared by the local Japanese residents, and later he ate heartily of his final dinner meal.

The new gallows had been erected in the yard under the kamani banyan tree. After the prisoners finished their dinner meal, all but those confined to death row cells were sent out of the prison on work details. Exactly at noon Gisaburo was conducted into Warden William Henry's office, where US Marshal Eugene R. Hendry read the death warrant and the record of appeals and respites, which were translated by J. H. Hakuole. Marshal Hendry then asked Gisaburo if he had anything to say and he replied, as translated, "Nothing in particular. I want to say that the warden, Mr. Henry, has been very good to me." All the witnesses were then directed into the yard, where they took their seats on the benches arranged about the gallows. The nine doctors in attendance stood near the gallows stairs.

A crowd of several hundred spectators had gathered outside the prison walls, but they could see nothing but the tops of the heads of those on the scaffold. Gisaburo, wrists bound behind, appeared at 12:15 p.m. led out by two native guards. He took his place on the trapdoor, where his arms, knees, and ankles were bound with straps while the guards supported him. The noose was then slipped over his head and cinched in place about his neck, and the black hood was pulled over his head. Gisaburo spoke and Reverend Motokawa translated, "He says wait a minute!" After a brief conference the black hood was pulled up to rest on top of Gisaburo's head and the noose was removed. The condemned man asked for the Bible from which the Reverend was about to read so he could read a particular passage. He read St. Matthews' story of the crucifixion in Japanese, repeating several times the portion relating to the execution of the two thieves. He stopped in his narrative to relate the details of the murder. Then he said, "I did not know then that it was wrong, but now I know my punishment is just, and I am prepared to die. I became a Christian in Japan when I was fourteen years of age and soon after that I shipped to Portland. In Portland my troubles commenced. If the captain on the vessel had treated me kindly then I would not be here now." He returned to reading the Bible but then continued, "I am glad I saved the life of the cook. When I was on the witness stand I told what was wrong, and I am glad now that the cook is not here. I had a fair judgment and all the people were good to me. I want to thank you all and I repent now. If I had been a Christian on December 26th I would have repented then. I did not know Christ then. I hope all my Japanese friends also know Christ." After Reverend Motokawa concluded the translation, he read Gisaburo's final statement.

Since I came here Chief Jailor Henry extended me his kindness and I feel very grateful of it. I thank you gentlemen who helped me in every way to this criminal. Since last December by the guidance of Reverend Mr. Motokawa, I am in belief of Almighty God, Jesus Christ the Savior, resurrection and everlasting life. I am now ready to go to death in peace. Dearly would I accept this salvation through your kindness which you extended to me to live longer in this world. I have no means to express my hearty thanks to Jailor Henry in this world but I hope to see him in another world.

The noose was then readjusted, but Gisaburo asked that his stiff collar be removed, as it was choking him. After the collar was removed, the noose was readjusted a third time. Then Gisaburo, in very good English, said, "Good-bye, everybody."

The black hood was pulled down over the prisoner's head at 12:31 p.m., as recorded by Deputy Chillingworth, and as Reverend Motokawa said his final Amen! the signal was immediately given by Marshal Hendry. The trapdoor was sprung as three electric buttons were pushed, two being dummies, and Gisaburo dropped four feet, breaking his neck in the fall. Prison physician Dr. Moore, assisted by Drs. Holt and Wilson, monitored Gisaburo's vital signs while the other six doctors observed or assisted, including Drs. Burgess, Hoffman, Hodgins, Oyama, Haida, and Mitamura. After fourteen minutes, at 12:45 p.m., the prisoner was pronounced dead. Five minutes later the body was cut down, placed in a coffin provided by the Japanese community, loaded into a hearse, and taken to the Japanese Christian Church. Following a brief service by Reverend Motokawa, the remains were driven to the Makiki cemetery and buried in the Japanese section. Later a rumor was spread among the Japanese that Gisaburo had been resuscitated, but an investigation proved the rumor false.

The schooner
Fred J. Wood
UNIVERSITY OF
WASHINGTON; SPE-
CIAL COLLECTIONS:
PH COLL 205; EDWIN
GARNER AMES
ALBUM, PG. 24

CHAPTER 14

Execution by Firing Squad

Peter Mortensen was born in Richfield, Utah, in 1865. In 1891 he was living in Ogden when he was suspected of arson. A man named Whitaker was arrested for the crime, tried, and acquitted, and Mortensen was the primary witness against him. Mortensen moved to Salt Lake City in 1897 and worked for the Pacific Lumber Company for eighteen months, then he struck out on his own and opened a business as a contractor and architect. By 1901 he was a teacher of theology at the Forest Dale ward meetinghouse and was married with four small children. Mortensen had experienced several bad business years and had gotten himself and his business deeply into debt, but 1901 had been a good year. He had a number of excellent contracts and had collected large sums from several clients. However, he could not put his money in the bank as several vigilant creditors had attachments on any deposits he made. One of his primary creditors was his old employer, the Pacific Lumber Company, to the sum of $3,879. Mortensen was particularly concerned about that debt because he could not continue in business if he could not get lumber for his jobs. On Monday, December 17, 1901, Mortensen went to the offices of the lumber company late in the afternoon and offered to pay $3,800 in gold coin on the account. He asked that someone come to his house that night to receive payment, and he required a signed receipt from the company's ledger. Company secretary James R. Hay agreed to pick up the money, but company manager George E. Romney adamantly instructed Hay not to pick it up at night but instead collect it in the morning. Hay then wrote out and signed the receipt and put it in his pocket. Hay and Mortensen, who had been friends for years, left together and took the streetcar back to their homes in Forest Dale. Apparently, while en route to Forest Dale, Mortensen convinced Hay to pick up the money that night, contrary to Romney's specific instructions.

James R. Hay had been born in Australia in 1870 and came to Salt Lake City, Utah, when he was sixteen years old. He was married in 1893 while he was working as a clerk for the Zions Cooperative Mercantile Institution, and in 1899 he took the position of secretary for the Pacific Lumber Company. Hay went straight home to his wife and four children living at 2211 Walnut Avenue. That night, after Hay ate supper with his family, he told his wife, "I have to go over to Brother Mortensen's for a few minutes to collect a large sum. I don't like to have so much money in the house overnight, but Brother Mortensen tells me that he must leave town early in the morning to be gone for a couple of days, he don't want to leave the money at his house and insists on paying it tonight." Hay told his wife to put their children to bed and not to wait up for him, and she followed his instructions.

Hay arrived at Mortensen's house about nine o'clock. Mrs. Mortensen had been visiting with her husband's sister-in-law, and they returned home together soon after Hay arrived. Seeing the men engaged in conversation, the women went into another room. Shortly after their return Mortensen and Hay left, but in a few minutes Mortensen returned and told his sister-in-law that he would now escort her home, which was only a short distance from the Mortensen house. Mrs. Mortensen retired as soon as her company left, but about an hour later she was awakened by the sound of a dog howling strangely. She saw that her husband had not yet returned, but he soon arrived and they retired. Later, Mrs. Mortensen would learn that the dog had started barking when a pistol shot rang out.

At 3:00 a.m. Mrs. Hay awoke and became concerned upon finding that her husband had not returned home. She dressed and hurried to the Mortensen home. The couple arose and told Mrs. Hay that they did not know where Hay was. Peter told Mrs. Hay that her husband had been concerned about having the large sum of money in his house overnight and may have taken it down to the office and then, it being such a late hour, he may have stayed over at some friend's house. When there was no sign of Hay the next morning, his friends and relatives began searching. Hay was known as an honest man so theories that he had defaulted were dismissed by most, and foul play or insanity was proposed as an explanation for his absence.

At 9:00 on the morning of December 19, Frank Torgersen was looking for a horse that had escaped from his pasture when he noticed blood on the Park City railroad tracks. There had been a rash of dog killings recently, and he decided to find the animal so he could notify the owner. He saw a mound of freshly dug dirt twenty-five yards from the track on the other side of a fence, so he went to James Hendry's store to borrow a pick. He carefully dug into the mound until he uncovered clothing, and then he quickly returned to the store for help. He found Royal B. Young and Peter Mortensen (who was still supposed to be out of town) waiting for the streetcar into the city, and he told them what he had found. They went to investigate but Torgersen, who refused to see the dead body he was sure was there, would not go with them. At the dirt mound they uncovered the body and recognized that it was Hay, so they pulled his overcoat over his face to protect it from animals and returned to the store. They told Torgersen to go back and guard the body, but he refused to go near a dead person, so Young went back while Mortensen called the police. The body was exhumed, and on examination it was seen that Hay had received a terrible blow to

Victim James R. Hay

SALT LAKE TRIBUNE: DECEMBER 19, 1901

his head from a sharp instrument. This was thought to be the cause of death until the autopsy revealed a bullet in Hay's brain. After finding the bullet the police secured Mortensen's pistol, a cheap model of a .32 caliber five-shot revolver. They found two chambers empty, two chambers loaded, and one chamber with an expended shell casing. Because of the time that had elapsed, they could not determine if the gun had been fired recently. The ball removed from Hay's brain was weighed and determined to be .32 caliber.

The police questioned Mortensen, the last man to see Hay alive. Mortensen said he had taken 190 twenty-dollar gold pieces he had stored in mason jars on a joist in his basement, put these into a bag, and paid them over to Hay just before he left the Mortensen house, and Hay had put the bag in the outside pocket of his overcoat. The first discrepancies immediately surfaced, as Hay's overcoat had no outside pockets and a careful search of the basement showed there was no joist as described. Heavy dust covered everything in the basement, including a few mason jars that had obviously not been moved in months. Slowly the police began to build a case against Mortensen, noting that he had never before made a payment in this manner, he had insisted on the receipt being written out and signed in advance, and he knew satisfaction of his debt to the lumber company would reestablish his credit. They determined it was possible their suspect could have had $3,800 in gold coin as the contractor had collected large checks recently and had turned them into twenty-dollar gold pieces to thwart his other creditors. The police continued their investigation and were interested to learn about all the footprints at the dirt mound grave, which unfortunately had all been obliterated by the three men who first uncovered the body. The police made a search around the Mortensen home and found a place at a nearby fence where a body had been laid on the ground, and then they documented a shoe track that matched Mortensen's rubber overshoes exactly. They

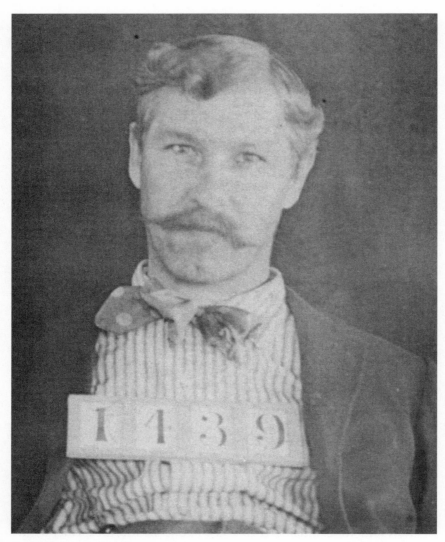

Peter Mortensen in prison

noted that the body had been hidden very close to Mortensen's home and that the murderer had made an unusual effort to hide the body so that it might look as if Hay had absconded with the funds. This was something a footpad would never have considered, and robbery was not the motive as Hay's watch and other personal belongings were still in his pockets and only his hat was missing. As the evidence mounted, Mortensen was arrested. Though the evidence was all circumstantial, it was strong by accumulation, and he was indicted on a charge of first-degree murder and tried at the spring term of the district court. The defendant was found guilty as charged and sentenced to die, and he chose the firing squad. The usual appeals followed, which stayed the execution, but the conviction and sentence of the lower court was finally affirmed, and the petition to the Board of Pardons for a commutation of Mortensen's sentence was denied.

On the night before his execution, the prisoner had an interview with Governor Heber M. Wells in the warden's office. General John Q. Cannon, Warden George N. Dow, Assistant Warden Wright, and a guard by the name of Naylor were also in attendance. A little after 10:00 p.m., the prisoner was returned to his cell at the east end of the cell block on the ground floor. Here two of his brothers, Henry and David, and his attorneys, B. J. and C. B. Stewart, waited, and they remained with him until after midnight. After they left the prisoner was still restless, so he talked with deathwatch guard W. C. A. Smoot until 2:00 a.m. He gave every minute detail of his interview with the governor, repeating himself often, until he became so hoarse he could hardly speak, and then he retired. He was asleep in minutes and slept soundly until 6:30 a.m. when Smoot woke him. Mortensen arose, washed, dressed in his burial clothes, and waited for his breakfast. He had not asked for anything in particular and then dallied with the food when it was served, eating very little. After breakfast, at 9:00 a.m., the death warrant was read to him and then his visitors began to arrive. First came his father, and then his brothers David and Jesse, his sister-in-law Lizzie, his brother Henry's son, and his two attorneys. He told his father that he wanted to be buried next to his mother and brother in Ogden without any religious service, and their parting at 9:30 a.m. was a touching affair, with hugs, kisses, and an abundance of tears from all the family present.

Mortensen had asked Warden Dow to send reporters from four local newspapers to interview him, and they visited next. The prisoner immediately apologized, saying he had not found the time to finish a letter he had been writing for them. He seemed to pose for the reporters, chose his words with thoughtful deliberation, and carefully modulated his voice to achieve the desired effect as the subjects changed during his interview. He complimented the officers for their treatment of him while in prison and singled out a number of guards and deputies and the warden for praise. He thanked and commended his attorneys for their work on his behalf, then concluded:

To the world I want to say, and I swear by the heavens above, by the earth beneath, and by all that I hold near and dear on this earth, that I am not guilty of that cowardly murder of my dearest friend. I ask, therefore, no man's pardon for aught that I may have done in life. I am confident that my life is an example to most people. I do not say that I am better or more worthy of the respect of the world than the average man, but I have done my duty to my friends, to my father and mother, to my brothers and sister and to my other near relatives. I have done my absolute duty toward my wife and my five little babies. May God keep and care for those sweet darlings. You who have hearts and feelings, and have families, I say to you to help them if you can.

Once Mortensen concluded his remarks, the reporters were escorted to the room at the end of the cell block. Shortly after ten o'clock the guards began to check tickets and admit the ninety-eight approved witnesses. They stepped between the double-steel gates in groups and were then admitted into the prison yard. They kept to the north of the buildings and walked past the large cell house to the end of the blacksmith shop, where they found themselves at the head of a passageway in which the death chair stood. It was a common wooden office chair with arms that was set on a low wooden platform. Behind the chair was a boxlike structure five feet high and two feet thick that was filled with dirt to catch the bullets after they passed through Mortensen's body. The crowd was kept behind a twisted wire barricade stretched from the building to the yard wall. As soon as all the witnesses were in place, the march down the jail corridor began. A prison guard was on one side of the prisoner, Dr. A. C. Young on the other, and, as they passed the cells, the prisoners exchanged their last good-byes. In the room at the end of the cells, the condemned man shook hands with the last of the reporters before they hurried out to the place of execution. Mortensen's hands were handcuffed behind his back, a white handkerchief was tied over his eyes, a white paper target was pinned over his heart, and he was led out of the jail by two deputy sheriffs. The prisoner could see nothing of the rifles or of the spectators as he was seated. His shoulders were strapped to the back of the chair, his forearms to the arms of the chair, and his legs to the cross support underneath the seat, and then the officers retreated a safe distance. The double doors to the blacksmith shop were propped open, and a blue denim curtain in which five portholes had been cut at about shoulder height had been hung over the opening. Five rifle barrels protruded from these portholes, and when Sheriff C. F. Emery gave the signal of "Ready, Aim, Fire!" all five erupted as one. There was no smoke, as smokeless powder was used, but a jet of flame could be seen coming from each barrel. Mortensen made a convulsive movement, his head slowly slumped forward, and his fingers twitched. Doctor

Young rushed forward and, grabbing a wrist, found that his pulse had ceased. The body was lifted onto a canvas stretcher and carried into the prison chapel. There Dr. Young examined the prisoner's remains and found that all four bullets, one rifle being loaded with powder only, had passed entirely through the body and entered the box behind. The shots were grouped no larger than a hand's breadth and were precisely on target.

Soon after the shooting a hearse hired by the Mortensen family arrived and made its way through the large crowd that had gathered outside the prison gate. As the "dead wagon" waited to enter, a closed carriage left the prison and the hearse had to be backed to let it pass. Inside the carriage were the five executioners, determined to remain anonymous. The remains of Peter Mortensen, as he had requested, were taken to Ogden and buried without ceremony.

CHAPTER 15

"I'll go to Hell sure."

Homer P. Ward lived alone in a cabin located between White Sulphur Springs and Neihart on Sheep Creek, several miles from any Montana settlement. He built a house and a barn and worked hard to improve his property. He had just invested a great deal of time and effort meticulously caulking the chinks between the logs with moss by driving it in with a wooden wedge and mallet, and the cabin was nearly airtight in preparation for Montana's severe winter weather. On November 21, 1904, Thanksgiving eve, twenty-eight-year-old Herbert Henry Metzger snuck up on the cabin, peeked through the east window, and found Ward seated at his table eating a meal, with his back toward the window. Metzger fired a single shot through the window pane, and the bullet struck Ward in the back of the head, killing him instantly. The shot put a small hole in the glass pane and blew parts of Ward's skull forward, including a small piece of skull and the leaden ball, which made another small hole in the west window pane directly opposite the east window. Metzger then entered the cabin, dragged and lifted the body onto the bed, and ransacked the cabin for valuables. He took a number of Ward's personal items, including Ward's hat, and discarded his own very distinctive hat on the floor of the cabin. He covered the body with old newspapers, saturated the bed, bedding, and body with kerosene, and then lit the pyre with a match before he fled. As he left the property, he set fire to a small barn as well. He was certain that the entire cabin, including the body and his hat, would be burned to ashes, hiding the crime and his identity. However, the cabin was so airtight that the fire quickly consumed all the oxygen, the fire was smothered, and Ward's body was blackened but not consumed. The fire created such a perfect vacuum that two kittens sleeping in a box beneath the stove were asphyxiated; the two bullet holes in the windows and the slight spaces around the door did not admit enough air to save them or fuel the flames. Ward's remains were discovered on Thanksgiving day. The bullet holes in the glass panes, the half-eaten meal, the bloodstains where the body fell and was dragged to the bed, the bits of skull and brain matter splattered about, the missing property, and all other circumstances told a story of murder for robbery. In the ashes the men found a .30-.30 shell casing, which curiously had not been discolored by the flames. Officers spent the next several days investigating but had developed no leads until a twelve-year-old boy living with Frank Petite identified the hat as belonging to Metzger. This fixed the crime on him, so Major James F. Keown of Bozeman, with Deputy Sheriffs George Williams and John Payne, left for the Belt Mountains where the fugitive had gone. They followed Metzger's trail to the camp of Alex Orict near Neihart, in the Little Belt Mountains, arriving on December 4, and in the cabin they found Ward's harness and bearskin coat. The lawmen detained Orict until Metzger arrived a few hours later, wearing Ward's hat and carrying Ward's rifle, and then both men were arrested.

Orict was quickly cleared of any complicity, as the work had clearly been done by one man, and Metzger's trial began at the Meagher County seat of White Sulphur Springs on March 23, 1905. The defendant testified in his own defense, and it may have been a slip of his tongue that convicted him. He insisted he had never been in Ward's cabin and said that Ward's hat had been given to him by a man he did not know whom he had met on the road a few miles from the Ward cabin. He said, "I tried the hat on and it was too small. I took the paper out of the hatband and threw it on the floor." When he tried to correct "floor" to "grass," it only drew attention to his faux pas. Metzger was convicted of first-degree murder, the jury deliberating only two hours, and he was sentenced by Judge Edwin K. Cheadle to hang on May 5, 1905. At Metzger's request his attorney did not file a motion asking for a new trial or an appeal, and Metzger refused to ask for a commutation of sentence or clemency in any form. Although he had no money and no friends in the area, he could have written to his family in Ohio for funds, but he refused. He insisted he was innocent and first tried to fix the blame on Orict. When that failed, he tried through innuendo to shift the blame to others. However, the circumstantial and physical evidence had been too conclusive, and his claims were dismissed.

By April 28 Sheriff C. H. Sherman had posted the invitations. As the date approached for the execution, Metzger had many visitors, but all those who came were merely curious and not particularly sympathetic. He spent his time smoking and chatting with his deathwatch guards. Undersheriff George Williams and he had developed a good rapport, and they exchanged anecdotes about hangings. Williams found Metzger crying one morning, but the prisoner insisted that he was only melancholy from thinking about his family, not his impending death. On Wednesday before the execution, the carpenter was busy assembling the gallows and erecting the high board fence that would provide privacy during the execution, and the sounds of hammer and saw visibly wore on the prisoner's nerves. The gallows was tested on Thursday and found to be in perfect working order. The hanging rope had been stretched for several days using a two-hundred-pound sack of sand, and this weight was also used in the testing. The rope where the noose was tied was lubricated using soap to ensure it would slide easily, and the pulleys were thoroughly oiled and checked.

The same gallows had been used to hang convicted murderer James Martin on February 23, 1904, at Butte in Silver Bow County. It was painted black and resembled the frame of a large gate as the upright timbers measured six by six inches and were twelve feet high. The crossbeam, ten feet in length, supported an iron pulley four feet from one end. Through this pulley a three-quarter-inch rope ran to another pulley directly against the post, and from there the rope ran down to connect to the massive weight. This weight, which measured only ten by seven by thirteen inches, weighed 310 pounds and was composed of lead encased in tin. The weight rested upon a piece of iron in the form of an oxbow or clevis, such as that used in the tongue of a plow, and worked like a lever on the post. The portion upon which the weight rested projected six inches, while the arm on the opposite side extended eighteen inches so that little tension was placed upon the restraining cord connected to a ring holding the weight in position four feet above the ground. The gallows frame was securely braced to the wall of the jail, and another brace was placed against the upright beam nearest the noose. The top of the frame was level with the twelve-foot-high jail building and positioned so that there was no view of the structure from any elevation outside the forty-two-foot-by-thirty-two-foot enclosure, and a railing had been built ten feet from the gallows to keep back the small crowd of witnesses. A canvas tent was pitched near the post that supported the weight so that the weight and release were concealed from view, thus keeping the identity of the person who activated the contrivance unknown. The executioner would spring the weight by cutting the restraining cord with a knife.

Two days before his execution, Metzger sent a note to Thomas Newman, a barkeep friend, saying, "Please fill this bottle with whiskey and charge it to my account. – Herbert H. Metzger." Newman, with characteristic generosity, opened an account on a clean page of his ledger and sent back word that the prisoner's credit was good until five o'clock Friday evening. That morning the prisoner was given a letter from his sister, Ida Young Pierce of Ohio, asking him to come home. He was not much affected by the note and wrote back saying nothing of his situation, and he gave his response to Reverend H. G. Wakefield of Lewistown to post. Wednesday evening three musicians went to the jail with banjo, guitar, and harmonica and played a number of tunes for the prisoner. One ragtime jig prompted Metzger to say, "I'll go to Hell sure if I keep pace with that." He became nearly hilarious and called out, "Let's have another drink."

Reverend Wakefield spent many hours with Metzger throughout his time in jail, though the condemned man did not support the clergy generally and thought them all hypocrites. On Thursday, May 4, the reverend arrived early to offer religious consolation, but Metzger refused to see him. The prisoner said, "I do not care to talk to him and I want no one to pray for me." However, he did agree to see a reporter who had promised to record and publish his statements. Metzger, as he had done before, tried to shift the blame to Alex Orict. He said he would have told his story on the witness stand but he feared that he would get a life sentence and preferred to hang. Later that morning two "women of the town," his only female sympathizers, visited, and they spent several hours in conversation. On the prisoner's last night, J. L. Dilworth sat with him until 3:00 a.m. discussing people they both knew in Canton, Ohio, and then Metzger retired. The prisoner arose at 7:00 a.m. and dressed for breakfast. After Metzger finished his meal, Sheriff Sherman held open house, and the prisoner talked with his many curious visitors. The jail closed for the noon meal, and Metzger ate a hearty chicken dinner. After that he napped on his cot. The sheriff woke the prisoner at 2:30 p.m. and read the death warrant. When the reading concluded Metzger said, "I never lose any sleep over a little thing like this, and I won't lose any hereafter. I feel sorry for the officers; they look like they are going to be hung. I felt like joking when the warrant was read." Undersheriff Williams then entered the cell and asked, "Well, Metzger, are you ready?" and he replied that he was. "Do you want a drink first?" he was asked, and he replied, "I don't give a damn!

Herbert Metzger prepared to be hanged by Deputy George Williams, with Dr.
Stephens looking on
AUTHOR COLLECTION

What have you there? Are you going to put a harness on me?" Metzger
took a drink and then put on his coat, and the leather belt was placed
around his waist. Metzger then said, "George, God bless you," and then,
"Good-bye, Sherman." He called for another drink and it was given,
the glass filled to the brim. While he was being prepared, a reporter
asked, "Have you anything you want us to say for you?" and the prisoner
replied, "Give my best wishes to those who have come to see me. A man
never knows who his friends are until he is in trouble." The reporter

Metzger hanging with Dr. J. M. Kumpe (left), Dr. Stephens (right), and Deputy Williams looking on
AUTHOR COLLECTION

asked him about the shiny shell casing found in the cabin, which had never been explained, and he replied, "Now it was strange that shell should have been found inside. The first thing a man would do who fired that shot would be to eject another cartridge into the magazine." The reporter suggested that possibly the shell caught in the murderer's clothing and was thus carried in. "No! No!" Metzger responded, adding, with another slip of the tongue, "I always wore a sweater up in the mountains there and it could not have caught in that."

The walk to the gallows was made quickly, and the condemned man took his place on the platform beneath the noose. The sheriff placed the noose over his head, positioned it behind his left ear, and cinched it tight to hold it in place. Undersheriff Williams, at the same time, applied the straps to the prisoner's ankles and knees, and then the black hood was pulled over Metzger's face. Sheriff Sherman immediately stepped behind the canvas, removing any doubt as to who would cut the restraining cord, and there was the sharp rap of the clevis followed by the sound of the weight striking the earth at 2:45 p.m. Coincidently, the school bell rang for the afternoon recess hour just as Metzger was jerked into the air and then fell back until his toes dangled eighteen inches above the platform. The body convulsed, his hands clenched and unclenched, and his shoulders drew upward, and Reverend Wakefield offered a prayer for the murderer's soul as his life ebbed away. Doctors J. M. Kumpe and John Stephens checked his pulse, and in eleven and one-half minutes they pronounced him dead. On careful examination it was determined that Metzger's neck had not been broken, but his spinal cord had been severed by the sudden jerk. A pine coffin, painted black with white metal handles, was brought forward. The body was cut down and deposited in it as the rope was being cut into pieces and distributed to the witnesses as souvenirs. Metzger's remains were interred in the city cemetery before sundown.

CHAPTER 16

The Brutal Murder of Amanda Youngblood

In 1901 Thomas M. and Amanda E. Youngblood left their home of many years in Sweetwater, Tennessee, and moved to Valverde, Colorado. They bought the grocery store located at 1275 Alameda Street and lived in three rooms at the rear with their thirty-year-old son Robert, along with his wife and four children. They put their life's saving into the store and were doing quite well. On December 31, 1903, sixty-four-year-old Thomas and sixty-three-year-old Amanda tried to stay up to see in the New Year, but by 11:15 p.m. they joined the rest of their family and retired. At 11:30 p.m. there came a loud knock at the side door. Thomas answered, and three men stood outside. They wanted to use the telephone to call for assistance for one of the men, who appeared ill, and Thomas admitted them. As soon as they were inside, two of the men pulled on masks. Thomas then noticed that the third man, the one pretending to be sick, was wearing a false beard. The masked men drew their pistols and ordered the old man to raise his hands, but Thomas refused. He was grabbed and thrown down onto the floor by the robbers, but he continued to resist. Amanda heard the scuffling and her husband's cries for help, so she rushed out of the bedroom while calling to her son, "Robert, come and save your father from being killed." As she reached the doorway to the store area, with Robert right behind her, one of the men fired. The bullet struck Amanda in the face, going through her mouth and coming out the back of her head; she bled to death in minutes. The second armed man also fired a shot, and this bullet struck Robert in his left cheek, causing a terrible wound and knocking him unconscious. Seeing the two people collapse badly wounded, the intruders abandoned their plan of robbery and fled, with Thomas following closely behind while calling for help and promising vengeance. The three younger men easily outran the older Youngblood, so all he saw, as he seemed to be catching up to them, was a buggy driving away on West Twelfth Street with the three murderers inside. The police surgeon was called to the scene. He pronounced Amanda dead, but when the surgeon found that Robert had a chance for life, he had the shooting victim hurriedly placed in an ambulance and rushed to the hospital. While being treated, Robert had to be held down by several men because, in his delirium, he seemed to be continuing his fight with the robbers.

The three men who had knocked at the Youngbloods' door were Charles O. Peters, Frederick Arnold, and Newton Andrews. Peters, a veteran of the Philippine war, had been born in West Dover, Ohio, in 1879. He had settled in Denver when he mustered out of the service. Arnold had been born in Omaha, Nebraska, in 1884 and was the husband of Robert Youngblood's half sister. Andrews had been born in Rochester, New York, in 1883 and had come to Denver in November 1903. Andrews was the chief plotter of the crime, and he fired the shot that killed Amanda. Arnold had fired the shot that wounded Robert, and Peters was the robber wearing the false beard and feigning sickness. The three murderers drove to a stable through streets thronged with New Year's revelers and seemed lost to any who might try to follow or trace them. They went to their quarters in the red-light district of Denver and then joined the celebrants in the saloons.

The police had few leads, so they began to arrest likely suspects. At 1:00 a.m. Peters and Andrews were arrested on suspicion as they were coming out of a saloon on Market Street, and the following day at noon Arnold was arrested at his Market Street home. No sooner had Arnold been lodged in jail than he broke down and confessed all the details of the attempted robbery, implicating Peters and Andrews. Arnold said he had told the others where they could find a lot of money, and he had a grudge to settle with his wife's half brother, Robert, who had tried to save his sister from the life of prostitution that supplied Arnold with money. As soon as Arnold confessed to being one of the robbers, he and Andrews confessed to firing the shots. Peters, however, insisted he had no weapon with him and had fired no shots, and the other two corroborated his assertion.

During the afternoon of January 1, word came to the police that there were threats of lynching from Valverde, so that night under cover of darkness the three murderers were moved to Colorado Springs. However, they were returned in time to be arraigned on January 9, and the three-day trial of Andrews and Peters began before Judge Peter I. Palmer on January 25 in the Westside criminal court. On January 27 both defendants were found "guilty of murder in the first degree, with the death penalty." The trial of Arnold began the following day, with the same result occurring on January 29. On February 8, 1904, Judge Palmer sentenced all three men to hang the week of May 15, but an appeal was filed with the state supreme court, which stayed the execution. On February 6, 1905, the conviction and sentence of the lower court was affirmed, and the execution was rescheduled for May 21. Petitions were then filed with the board of pardons and denied for Andrews and Arnold, but Peters was reprieved on a plea of insanity. Arnold and Andrews were granted a three-week respite so an appeal could be filed with the US Supreme Court. That high court refused to grant a writ of habeas corpus, and the date for execution was then set for the week of June 14, 1905. Petitions for a commutation of sentence to life imprisonment followed and were denied for Andrews and Arnold, but Peters was reprieved until November 19 and admitted to a hospital. Next the mothers of the condemned men were graciously received by Governor Jesse F. McDonald. However, though he was sympathetic to their situation, he refused to intervene. During their final days both prisoners received visits from their mothers. Andrews was touched by his mother's misery, but Arnold was cold, almost brutal, to his mother and to other family members who came to visit. Neither mother gave up hope for some intervention until notified on June 17, 1905, that the executions had taken place the previous evening.

The gallows, the "automatic suicide machine," could accommodate only one man at a time, and it was decided that Andrews would go first. During the late afternoon hours, witnesses began arriving at the prison gate. They were admitted into the warden's office until the hour of execution drew near, and then they were escorted to the death house in the northeast corner of the prison yard. The doors to the cells of the two condemned men had been covered with curtains before the witnesses were conducted through the weight room into the execution chamber. Once the witnesses were in place, the curtains were removed and Warden John Cleghorn went to Andrews's cell to read the death warrant and record of appeals and respites. The prisoner's arms were strapped to his body, and his wrists were strapped behind him. At 8:00 p.m. he was escorted the twenty-five feet from his cell into the death chamber, where he took his place inches in front of the spring-loaded platform. Andrews stated that he was innocent of murder and had fired one shot into the ceiling, argued that Arnold alone was guilty of murder for revenge, and accused the state of murdering him. When he concluded, the prison chaplain began a prayer and Andrews dropped to one knee, his eyes moist, and several sobs escaped his lips. When the chaplain said "Amen," the prisoner arose. His knees and ankles were quickly strapped, the noose was positioned, and the black hood was pulled over his head. Warden Cleghorn and a guard lifted Andrews onto the center of the platform, and all eyes, save those of the prisoner, turned to the dial on the wall. When Andrews heard the water running, as it drained from the upper bucket of the water release, he called out, "Oh, Lord God, have mercy on my soul. Oh God, receive my soul." At 8:22 p.m. the weight of water in the upper bucket was reduced to eleven pounds, the bucket shifted, and the iron rod was sprung, releasing the twenty-five-pound iron ball, which fell onto the trigger releasing the three-hundred-pound weight. The heavy weight dropped into a tray of sawdust, which muffled the sound, and Andrews was jerked five feet into the air. Doctors W. L. Davis and T. D. Palmer recorded Andrews' pulse, and at 8:37 p.m. they pronounced him dead. The body was quickly removed to the morgue, and the chamber was cleaned and readied for Arnold. In the weight room the upper bucket was refilled and the lower one emptied, the weight was raised, and the trigger mechanism was reset.

A few minutes before 9:00 p.m., Warden Cleghorn read the death warrant and record of appeals and respites to Arnold. After his arms were strapped to his body and his wrists strapped behind him, he was escorted twenty-five feet into the death chamber. As he stood at the platform, he was asked if he had anything to say. His reply was, "I was never given a fair chance, and I am innocent of this murder. This is simple murder by the state." When it was clear he had concluded his brief remarks, his knees and ankles were strapped, the noose was adjusted and cinched in place, and the black hood was pulled over his head. As he was lifted and placed onto the center of the spring-loaded platform by Warden Cleghorn and a guard, he said through the black cloth, "Good-bye Warden." Warden Cleghorn replied, "Good-bye, son." The same process ensued, and the great weight fell at 9:07 p.m. Arnold was pronounced dead nine minutes later.

Arnold's remains joined those of Andrews's in the prison morgue. Both bodies were taken to the prison's operating room for autopsies, as required by law, while the witnesses signed the death certificate and then filed out of the chamber. The autopsies were performed by acting

Frederick Arnold
DENVER DAILY NEWS: JUNE 17, 1905

Newton Andrews
DENVER DAILY NEWS: JUNE 17, 1905

prison physician Dr. T. D. Palmer, assisted by Dr. M. A. Thompson of Chicago and Dr. W. L. Davis of Denver, with Dr. Singer of Pueblo as a witness to the procedures. The examinations showed that in both bodies the necks had been broken by the jerk, and the surgeons insisted that neither realized what was happening after the first tightening about their necks. The body of Andrews was delivered to his mother, and she took his remains to Denver for burial. Arnold's family had left town before the execution, so his remains were interred in the prison cemetery the following day.

Charles O. Peters, who was sentenced to die in November, was in the hospital and unable to comprehend events. His health was deteriorating rapidly, and doctors did not think he would live until the fall. Peters died before he could be executed for his part in the murder of Amanda Youngblood.

CHAPTER 17

Carnage in the Desert

The Hancock brothers—John, Walter M., and Thomas R.—lived in the Southern California area at the end of the nineteenth century. In 1890 John Hancock committed a burglary. He was arrested, convicted, and sentenced to serve a year at San Quentin prison, where he was registered as prisoner No. 14315. After his release he continued to commit petty crimes and served several brief sentences in jail. About 1894 he met Winifred "Winny" Myers, a married woman with a six-year-old son but no husband present, and they began living together. In 1896 Hancock bought a horse and buggy at Riverside, making a down payment of ten dollars on the horse and five dollars on the buggy, but he "skipped with them," never paying the balance. He, Myers, and her son then went to live on the ranch of Mrs. Pease near El Modena, six miles west of Orange. Hancock agreed to work the place and provide a home for Mrs. Pease for one year, and he converted a wagon bed into a box that could hold a dozen or more chickens. Accompanied by Herbert Carter, who was renting the adjoining ranch, Hancock would drive the wagon toward Los Angeles or Santa Ana at 3:00 or 4:00 p.m. each afternoon and return about midnight, and the box would be filled with stolen chickens. They kept at it for months until there were more than five hundred stolen chickens on the Pease and Carter ranches. While stealing the chickens the pair would take anything else of value lying at hand, including quite a supply of stolen harness. Carter soon tired of the petty criminal life, and Charles Knox took his place. After two more months of stealing chickens, Hancock, in April 1897, "jumped his contract" with Mrs. Pease. He and Myers, with Myers's son, started from El Modena, California, for Salt Lake City, Utah.

Hancock had not managed to sell much of his plunder and had little money, so they were traveling in a miserable excuse for an outfit drawn by four inferior horses. One of their animals gave out at Daggett, California, but Hancock acquired another "plug" and continued on. When they could go no farther, Hancock took a job at a Pahrump, Nevada, ranch to earn enough money to improve their condition and continue their journey. Three weeks after Hancock arrived in Pahrump, Dr. George Engelke, a veterinary surgeon, and Peter "Joe" Edmiston, his driver, arrived from Los Angeles, California, driving a first-class outfit drawn by a fine team. They also had with them a fine racehorse named Chief and two bloodhounds. They were on their way to Ogden, Utah, where Engelke planned to make a surprise visit to his sister and mother, whom he had not seen in years. Engelke shared his plans with Hancock, and the latter decided to travel with Engelke. Before he quit and left the ranch, Hancock stole a fully loaded six-shooter from a dresser drawer in the main house.

Hancock stewed over Engelke's disclosure that no one expected him at Ogden and how the doctor had bragged that he had been quite successful in Los Angeles. The third day on the trail, May 18, Hancock said, "Winny, I'm broke, and I think that Engelke has a lot of money on him. I'm going to kill them, take their money and their team, and leave ours on the desert." Myers later claimed that she had protested vehemently, but Hancock threatened that he would murder her and abandon her son in the desert if she interfered or tried to warn his intended victims. Myers continued to plead with him not to commit murder, and he seemed to weaken in his resolve. That evening Engelke chose a campsite, but Hancock encouraged them to go on until they found a secluded spot in a small basin surrounded by sand dunes, twenty miles south of Eisemann's ranch in Lincoln County, Nevada. The wagons were positioned six feet apart, and all parties turned in early. Engelke and Edmiston slept near their wagon, and Myers, her son, and Hancock retired near theirs. Hancock often checked on the animals during the night, so Myers was not concerned when Hancock arose a little before 3:00 a.m. However, a peculiar noise aroused her, and she saw Hancock standing over their traveling companions with an axe in hand, and both men were bleeding from head wounds. He had crushed their skulls with the blunt end of the axe, but the men were not dead, so Hancock pulled his stolen revolver and shot each man twice. When they continued to moan, he pounded and slashed at them with the blunt and sharp edge of the axe until they were dead. The dogs then went to the dead men and began sniffing about and licking at the wounds, so Hancock used his last two bullets to kill them, one bullet each. He then searched the men's mutilated bodies. From the doctor he took a silver watch and chain, a pocket knife, a magnifying glass, a silk handkerchief, and a bank book showing he had on deposit several hundred dollars; while from Edmiston he took twelve dollars in currency.

Hancock ordered Myers to help him remove their personal belongings from their old wagon and to assist in rolling the men's bodies into cotton quilts. She was then required to help lift the bodies of the men and dogs into their old wagon. She later said she helped him because she did not want her son, who had remained asleep throughout the commotion, to wake up and see the carnage. Hancock drove the old wagon some distance from the camp, and when he returned with the old wagon, he told Myers he had buried the remains. He then went through all the goods in both wagons, taking everything they could use or sell and packing it into the good outfit. After putting the rest into their old outfit, Hancock released his horses, which were not worth the trouble to herd along, and then set his old outfit on fire before they started for Salt Lake City. At Pioche, Nevada, they stopped and Hancock sold the racehorse and some of the personal effects stolen from the deceased, as the only money they had was Edmiston's twelve dollars.

Hancock and Myers traveled together for more than a year after the murders, first to Salt Lake City, then to Portland, Oregon, and finally back into Southern California. Hancock always introduced Myers as his wife, though it appears he did not claim her son as his. During this time Myers tried repeatedly to get away from Hancock, but he kept a close watch on her every move and became increasingly suspicious and abusive. In California, when their funds ran low, Myers was forced to find a job, and she was employed at the Santa Fe oil wells in Fullerton. One day Hancock went to her place of employment and attacked her after a vicious argument. A coworker by the name of Gross took her part and received a serious gash from Hancock's knife for his chivalry. Hancock fled to avoid arrest, giving Myers the opportunity she had hoped for. She quickly left Hancock and moved in with Gross. Myers claimed that she married her rescuer, and they took up residence on Main Street in Los Angeles as husband and wife, along with her son. When the "bride" told her new husband of the horrible murder, he encouraged her to confess; she dutifully did as her new husband wanted.

Once Hancock learned that his former mistress had confessed all the details of the two murders to the authorities, he burglarized a store in Santa Ana, Orange County, California, hoping to get a stake for his escape. However, he was quickly arrested and indicted. To avoid extradition to Nevada, he pled guilty to a burglary he had committed three years earlier, before the facts of the murder and his arrest came to light in Nevada. His brothers claimed that Mrs. Gross was "an adventuress," her story was nothing but a lie to get revenge upon their brother John, and John had pled guilty falsely to avoid more serious trouble. John was supposed to be taken to Fullerton and charged with assault to commit murder on Mr. Gross, but when the charge was reduced to assault with a deadly weapon he was left in Santa Ana, where Judge Ballard sentenced him to serve ten years in prison. This satisfied Mr. and Mrs. Gross, so they did not pursue further criminal action. On November 28, 1898, Hancock was at the Southern Pacific railroad depot awaiting transfer to San Quentin prison, where he arrived on December 1, 1898, and was registered as prisoner No. 17976. By then extradition proceedings had been initiated by the Nevada authorities, but California governor James Budd refused to surrender the prisoner until he served out his sentence in California. When his prison term ended, Hancock was discharged on June 1, 1905, right into the waiting hands of Nevada lawmen who took him to Pioche for prosecution on the double-murder charge. Hancock told Sheriff H. E. Freudenthal where the bodies were buried and even provided a map. His description was so accurate that the sheriff, who was familiar with that desolate area, was able to unearth the larger bones and the skulls, which had survived the coyotes and the ravages of time buried in the desert. These remains showed where the men's heads had been crushed, slashed, and shot, and the sheriff took the remains to Pioche as evidence and for a Christian burial.

At his trial Hancock tried to prevent Mrs. Gross from testifying against him based upon the privilege of husband and wife, but testimony proved that she had never married Hancock. In fact there is no record of her marriage to Mr. Gross, and it appears she could not marry as she had a husband, alive and well, in another city. Mrs. Gross's testimony, along with Hancock's previous statements and the physical evidence, convicted Hancock, and he was sentenced to hang. The usual appeals and application for a commutation of sentence were quickly denied.

In 1901 the state legislature had ordered, beginning in 1903, that all legal executions be conducted in Nevada's state prison, but none had been conducted for two years. No funds had been authorized for construction of a gallows, but one was constructed at the south end of the shoe shop where the walls were thick, whitewashed stone and the ceiling high. A strip of carpeting was laid from the door to the foot of the gallows stairs, and seats were arranged for prison officials. On September 8, 1905, thirty-nine invited spectators were admitted through the prison gate, two by two, to witness the first execution in the prison. On the evening before the execution, the condemned man was administered the rite of baptism by Reverend B. J. Darneille in the presence of Nevada governor John Sparks, Warden J. L. Considine, the lieutenant of the guard, and his deathwatch officers. The religious ceremony had the effect of bracing up the prisoner, and he slept peacefully throughout the night. In the morning Hancock ate a hearty breakfast of oysters and then requested a walk outside his cell. He was especially interested in the prehistoric footprints that had been found in the prison's quarry, and he was permitted to examine them under close guard. Upon his return to the prison, he was seated in an easy chair. His wrists were shackled as he awaited the walk to the scaffold, and he showed no sign of nervousness. The condemned was dressed in a salt-and-pepper coat, a matching vest, and dark trousers, and his shoes were carefully shined. A large white chrysanthemum was inserted in his buttonhole, and by his chair was a bouquet of the same flower. Reverend Darneille remained by his side throughout the long wait, conversing with him as a friend and brother rather than as a clergyman. The condemned man took delight from his own humor, which grated upon the nerves of the others present, including a representative of *The News,* the officers of the guards, W. C. Nofsinger, James Sullivan, and George Siebert.

When the moment arrived for their walk to the scaffold, Warden Considine and Reverend Darneille led the procession. The condemned man followed closely, with his arms pinioned to his body, his wrists bound behind him, and his head bowed. He was followed closely by three guards in case he faltered or hesitated. He seemed unconcerned until he lifted his eyes and saw the noose dangling. He paused and asked to see the audience, and when the warden hesitated for a moment he claimed it as his right. He was then allowed to slowly scan the faces, making several faint signs of recognition to this man or that, until he saw Dr. W. L. Berry. He leaned forward and whispered some remark that destroyed the doctor's composure and caused him to cry uncontrollably. The condemned man then ascended the stairs with a firm step and stood upon the trapdoor. The warden held the death warrant, but Hancock waived the reading, so Drs. J. J. Circe and S. J. Sullivan of Virginia City hurriedly joined Dr. Berry beneath the scaffold. Doctor Circe was to assist Dr. Berry while Dr. Sullivan was to record all the details, but Dr. Circe took control of the situation when it seemed clear that Dr. Berry could no longer manage the determination of death.

After prayers were offered, the condemned's knees and ankles were pinioned, the black hood was pulled over his head, and the noose was slipped on and cinched firmly around Hancock's neck to keep it in the proper position. The Reverend then delivered the benediction ending with, " . . . and may God have mercy on your soul," to which Hancock replied impatiently, "He will! He will!" Within a moment after the condemned spoke, at 10:41 a.m., the trapdoor was sprung. The body dropped and immediately appeared limp and lifeless, without a visible twitch or quiver, and Hancock swung about slowly. Everyone watched Hancock's clenched hands, as he had said that if he was conscious he would relax one of his hands after the trapdoor fell, but both hands remained clenched. Doctor Circe quickly grabbed and steadied the body, immediately placed his ear to Hancock's chest, and reported that there was no heartbeat. However, within a few seconds a pulse returned and fluctuated for six minutes, and it was thirteen minutes before Dr. Circe pronounced Hancock dead. The body was allowed to hang a few minutes more, to ensure he could not be revived, and then it was cut down and deposited into the coffin that had been stored beneath the gallows. A postmortem examination, as required by law, revealed that the prisoner's neck had been dislocated at the first cervical vertebra. Following the examination the body was delivered to a funeral parlor and prepared for burial. On Saturday the funeral service was conducted according to the ritual of the Episcopal Church, with the casket surrounded by flowers donated by the prisoners, and interment followed in the prison's burial ground at 1:00 p.m.

John Hancock, Winifred "Winny" Myers, and victims Dr. George Engelke and Peter "Joe" Edmiston
SAN FRANCISCO CHRONICLE: DECEMBER 2, 1898

CHAPTER 18

Swift Justice in South Dakota

On July 5, 1909, John F. Ronayne and his fourteen-year-old son Michael were hoeing potatoes on a plot of land not far from fifty-six-year-old J. W. Christie's farm near Rudolph, several miles southwest of Aberdeen in southwest Brown County, South Dakota. Christie, a grain buyer, had rented the farm, and his family—sixty-year-old Mrs. Christie and thirteen-year-old daughter Mildred—lived in the small, ugly cottage on the farm while their home was being built in town. Michael Ronayne had spent the previous winter with the Christie family so he could attend school in the country, and John Ronayne usually put up his horses at the Christie place while working in the potato field. When it was time to go home, John Ronayne was hitching his team to his wagon when Christie suggested that Michael and his father spend the night so they would be fresh for work early the next morning, but John could not stay and returned to town. In the morning John drove his wagon and team into the fenced yard at the Christie place expecting to be met by Christie or his son, but the place was eerily quiet. He later said that he supposed the two men had gone to the grain elevator in Rudolph and that the women were still asleep in the house. It was just 7:00 a.m. when John went to the house and found Mrs. Christie lying in a pool of blood in the doorway between the small porch and the kitchen, shot through the body and dead. Mildred was lying on her bed, her bed clothes ripped from her body and a fatal bullet hole in her forehead, but there were no marks to suggest a further violation or outrage of the pretty young teenager. John then hurried to the barn and from the door he could see his dead son lying on his face in the dirt inside an empty stall. He went to him and found that he had been shot and his head had been crushed with a hammer, which lay nearby. He looked further and in the next stall, just behind the cow, he found Christie shot through the head, and his hat with a bullet hole through it lay beside the body. The murderer had apparently used the same hammer he later used on Michael to also crush Christie's head. The scene showed that Christie had been milking the cow when murdered and the evidence suggested that Michael must have come at the sound of the shot and been killed next. Mrs. Christie was making breakfast and it appeared, upon hearing two gun shots, she rushed out with the stove lifter still in her hand and met the murderer at the door, who placed the muzzle of his six-shooter against her body and fired. The murderer then went to the bedroom of Mildred, who put up quite a struggle, and she was the last to die. On the floor of Mildred's bedroom were four .41 caliber shells and one bullet, which the murderer had dropped as he reloaded his pistol. When John investigated further, it became clear that the house had been carefully ransacked and every bureau drawer, box, and purse had been gone through. Even the mattresses and rugs had been pulled apart. Still, in his haste, the murderer had left a five-dollar bill inside one purse and a gold watch lying in plain view in a dresser drawer.

Ronayne saw a crew working on the railroad and rushed to them for help. Crew foreman Mike Graff went back to the house with the grieving father, and they summoned the authorities. Brown County Sheriff John Anderson found tracks leading from the Christie farmhouse toward Mellette, and he heard that Emil Victor had been seen in the area. Victor had worked as an elevator handyman at the Rudolph grain elevator run by John Morrow, where Christie also worked. Victor knew Christie often carried large sums of money, and he had even remarked to other workmen how easy it would be to rob Christie. Sheriff Anderson discovered that Victor was heading toward Northville in northwest Spink County, so the sheriff started for Mansfield in J. F. Zietlow's Ford automobile. Once he arrrived in Mansfield, he telephoned Marshal Alden Wilson at Northville. When Emil Victor came into town, the marshal found him at the barbershop being shaved and arrested him. The prisoner was searched at the jail, and the deputies found in his pockets a man's gold watch, a man's penknife, a lady's penknife, an ordinary rough knife, books of one- and two-cent stamps, a Chatelaine pin brooch, a cameo pin brooch, a bar pin brooch, a pocketbook filled with change, and thirteen dollars in one- and two-dollar bills.

From the moment of his arrest, Victor began talking, but he related several conflicting stories. Victor was a middle-aged man of medium height and weight with a sandy complexion, light hair, and blue eyes. Two strangers had also been seen in the area, one short and fat with a moustache and the other light, smooth-faced, and taller, but they were found, questioned, and cleared of involvement. Victor insisted that he would also be cleared and said he could provide an alibi. He said he ate breakfast at Conde in northeast Spink County on Saturday morning and took the train to Northville, talking with the conductor about work at Northville. Victor also claimed his father was a successful dry goods merchant in Buffalo, New York, and he was well known there. But all he professed proved to be lies when investigated. In fact, Victor had come to South Dakota from East Aurora, New York, where he left behind his father, mother, and a younger sister. His father traveled to Aberdeen when he heard of his son's arrest, but at the time he had no money to hire an attorney and returned home.

The bodies of the murder victims were taken to Wilson's undertaking parlor in Aberdeen, and an inquest was held by county coroner George E. Countryman. Sheriff Anderson was the second witness, after John Ronayne, and he told how a watch had been torn out of the trouser buttonhole of Christie when the two men were searched by the murderer. He produced three bullet casings and one cartridge recovered from the floor in Mildred's bedroom, where the murderer had dropped them as he reloaded his pistol. The watch found with Victor was identified as Christie's by jeweler D. G. Gallett of Aberdeen, but he could not identify the brooches; the man's penknife was also identified as belonging to Christie. Gallett had sold the watch to Christie and kept a record by serial number. Morrow, who had been Victor's employer, said his men told him that the prisoner had boasted how easy it would be to rob Christie, but he said he had not personally heard the boast. Others testified that it was common knowledge Christie often carried cash in his long wallet so he could make purchases of grain if a deal presented itself.

On June 24 Victor had gone to the office of the *American* newspaper and expressed an interest in having his name in print. He was so anxious that it be printed by a certain date that he paid the advertising rate in advance. The following story, believed to be an effort to establish an alibi, was printed on June 25:

EMIL VICTOR GOES EAST
Eastern Man Here for a Year
Returning Home to Gather
Material for Airship

Emil Victor who has been working on the 2300 acre farm of John Morrow at Rudolph arrived here Wednesday and remained until Friday, the guest of Aberdeen friends, leaving for Northville yesterday, where he will spend a week. From Northville Mr. Victor will go to Chicago for a visit with his brother, and from there to Buffalo, N. Y. where his parents reside, his father being a proprietor of one of the leading dry goods stores in that city.

Mr. Victor came west about a year ago and is delighted with the country. He will spend the summer months in the east and will return next fall. He has been inspecting considerable land in this vicinity, and will make some purchases upon his return. He also intends registering for the Cheyenne reservation opening that will take place in the fall.

Mr. Victor has invented a flying machine and has plans drawn up for its construction. He will busy himself this summer in the east gathering materials and will complete building of the flyer here upon his return so that the trial flights will be made upon the Dakota prairies. Mr. Victor has a host of friends in South Dakota who are hopeful for the success of his invention.

Victor was held on a charge of murder and indicted by the grand jury. His special term trial began in the district court on August 24, and his court-appointed attorneys, John Ruckman and J. M. Lawson, presented a defense of insanity at the time the killing was done. The Victor family did not like the way his court-appointed attorneys were handling the case, so they hired C. R. Jorgensen to represent their son. Nevertheless, Victor was convicted of murder in the first degree and sentenced to hang on November 16, 1909. His family could not be present on his final day but had made arrangements for his burial. A few days before his execution, Victor received a letter from his family bidding him farewell, and his mother sent a five-dollar money order to his attorney asking him to make one last appeal to Governor Samuel H. Elrod for a stay of execution. She apologized that it was all she had because her garden had been neglected while she tried to save her son. He returned the money and explained that no effort would be successful at that late hour and assured her that every effort had already been made, but in vain.

On his last night the condemned man spent his time writing letters to his relatives and to several acquaintances he had made in Rudolph, then he retired. He spent a restless night but finally fell asleep shortly after midnight. At an early hour Sheriff Anderson woke him to hear the death warrant read. Victor arose to find Deputies Reese Price and Art Wagner on duty as his deathwatch guards, Deputies Dick Cameron and Vilas Quinn having been relieved while he slept. A small crowd of a dozen curious men had gathered in front of the jail at midnight. They remained through the cold, snowy night because they had heard a rumor that the execution might occur at 2:00 a.m., and they were still waiting there at sunrise. After the death warrant was read, Reverend F. J. Graeber, pastor of St. Paul's German Lutheran Church in Rudolph, spent time with the prisoner consoling him and praying for his salvation. The reverend had been attending to Victor's religious needs from his first day in jail, taking over the duty rather suddenly from another clergyman who had become quite ill and could not perform those duties. The prisoner was brought out of the jail after 7:30 a.m. wearing a black shroud over his entire body, hiding the straps that tightly bound his arms to his body and his wrists behind him, but the straps on his legs were loosely applied so he could walk. He bid farewell to his deathwatch guards before he was led through the door into the jail yard, the knee straps making his progress difficult. First came Sheriff Anderson, then the prisoner between Deputies Price and Cameron, and behind him were Deputies Henry Moulton and Art Walker. Deputy Jerry Castleton of Sioux Falls and the reverend stood nearby in case they were needed.

The scaffold had been erected on the north side of the jail yard within a high enclosure, and inside the tall board fence were twenty-five witnesses. They included lawmen, county and state officials, clergymen, doctors, and newsmen, and all wore heavy overcoats and shuffled about to keep warm as they stood in the snow. The prisoner was halted at the foot of the gallows stairs and there he was allowed to make his speech, but he said nothing of significance. However, when halfway up the stairs, he suddenly turned to the crowd and called out, "God forgive

Emil Victor
GABBIE HIRSCH

me for my sins and bless you all!" He then walked onto the platform and positioned himself in the center of the trapdoor. The straps were quickly tightened about his knees and ankles, and the noose was placed over his head. The black hood was drawn over his head and then the noose was positioned and cinched tight to hold it in place. In but a moment, at 8:09 a.m., the trapdoor was sprung by the sheriff and Victor dropped, breaking his neck in the fall. Coroner Dr. Countryman, assisted by Drs. R. D. Adams and R. L. Murdy, recorded the dying man's pulse, and in sixteen minutes pronounced Victor dead. After hanging a few minutes more, to ensure he could not be revived, the body was cut down, placed in a casket, and given in charge of undertaker Wilson. The undertaker saw that the family's funeral arrangements were fulfilled, and the body was buried in the Riverside Cemetery with a service performed by Reverend Graeber.

CHAPTER 19

The Wife Murderer

Twenty-eight-year-old Richard Quinn and his wife, Margaret, had domestic difficulties long before they left Michigan for North Dakota in 1904 and later moved to Washington in 1907. However, it seemed the difficulties had all been resolved when, in 1908, they settled at Everett, the Snohomish County seat. Quinn found work as a fireman at the Ferry-Baker Mill but lost that position, and in September he was working in the woods sawing shingle bolts. These setbacks led to more arguments, and Margaret complained to friends that Richard drank too much, abused her, and often threatened to shoot her. Finally, on August 1 Margaret left her husband for the second time since arriving in Washington, and she moved into the "Purdy House" run by Sadie Bond at 2920 Norton Avenue. She found work as a domestic for a widower with three children, but on September 15 she found a more permanent position at a restaurant and was determined to make her own way.

Richard was just as determined to disgrace his wife, and he made disparaging remarks about her to anyone who would listen. On September 17 Richard was seen riding his horse back and forth near the intersection of Summit Avenue and Twentieth Street, near his home, as if he expected his wife to make an appearance. That evening he was in the Rainier Saloon, and, strangely for those modern times, he was carrying his rifle. He threatened to shoot his wife but no one took him seriously, as he had made similar threats on many previous occasions, but nothing had ever happened. On September 18 Richard Quinn telephoned Margaret and told her to come for her trunk, threatening to throw it out if she did not come immediately. Margaret started for their home near the Ferry-Baker Mill. When she reached the intersection of Twentieth Street and Summit Avenue, Quinn appeared on horseback. He rode up, dismounted with rifle in hand, and said, "Good-bye, Maggie," then he shot her at such close range that the blast from the muzzle set her clothes afire. The bullet passed entirely through her body, entering near the center of her breasts and ranging downward until it pierced her abdomen and came out her back between the tenth and eleventh ribs. Later, at the autopsy, coroner Challacombe determined that this bullet had pierced the pericardium, the membrane that encloses the heart, passed through the liver and diaphragm, and shattered the spleen before exiting.

William Watts, a neighbor of the Quinns, heard the shot and a woman's scream. He ran outside and saw Richard standing with bridle in hand, watching his wife stagger along the sidewalk toward James C. Devery's home at 2006 Summit Avenue. Mrs. Quinn went through the gate onto Devery's porch and collapsed in a sitting position. Watts yelled at Richard, which seemed to startle him. Richard quickly mounted and rode off, and Watts returned to his home to get his rifle. When Watts returned to the scene of the shooting, he found that Richard, still mounted, had also returned and was trying to take aim at his wife. Watts pointed his rifle at Richard and threatened to shoot if he fired again, so Richard galloped down Twentieth Street. Immediately after the shooting, a report reached the police station that Richard Quinn had barricaded himself in his house and would defy the officers; but within an hour, before a force of officers could be assembled and dispatched, Quinn arrived at police headquarters accompanied by brother-in-law Bert Mason and surrendered. Quinn was placed in a patrol wagon and taken to the county jail at Everett, and he begged the patrolman to sit close to him so he could not be shot while in transit. Quinn's friends and relatives then came forward and asserted that Margaret Quinn had a gun and had threatened to shoot her husband. Though Richard claimed the shooting was accidental, they said it may have been in self-defense.

Margaret's room and belongings were searched, and it was proved she had no gun. Her friends testified that she had never threatened her husband and was afraid of him. As Margaret sat on Devery's porch, doctors and an ambulance were summoned. The physicians decided that their patient would bleed to death if driven to the hospital, so she was taken to a nearby house and given opiates to ease the terrible pain. It first appeared that she would die within hours, but by that evening she had rallied. It was briefly thought she might survive, but she continued to weaken. After continuing examination and treatment, the doctors determined that the wound was a mortal one and it was just a matter of time until Margaret died. Margaret was conscious and gave an antemortem statement naming her husband as her murderer. But she could not name any particular reason for the shooting beyond the couple's continuing marital difficulties. Margaret lingered until September 23, when she died a few minutes before 1:00 a.m. Her husband was asleep at the jail and was told of her death when he awoke. He showed no emotion, asking only if he could see her body before she was buried. Margaret Quinn was buried the following day, but Richard was not permitted to attend the funeral.

Quinn was indicted in early December, and his trial began in Judge W. W. Black's courtroom on December 14, 1908. His defense that the shooting was accidental was rejected by the jurors, and a claim of self-defense was not put forth. After two days of trial and brief deliberations, Quinn was convicted of first-degree murder. The prisoner was sentenced to hang, but appeals automatically stayed the execution until the state supreme court could hear the case. The justices finally denied the appeal and affirmed the conviction and sentence, and Quinn was re-sentenced to hang on April 15, 1910. Efforts were then made to obtain a commutation of the death sentence, or at least a reprieve, and Quinn's sister Mrs. Bert Mason, who lived in Everett, managed to get a twenty-eight-day reprieve from Governor M. E. Hay while the case was taken under consideration. Quinn's sister worked night and day until, at seven o'clock on the evening of May 12, the governor denied the application even though Mrs. Mason had submitted petitions signed by five hundred residents of Everett, including eleven of the twelve jurors who found her brother guilty.

Quinn was delivered to the prison at Walla Walla to await the date of his execution. He was registered as prisoner No. 5661 and lodged in the east wing of the cell block. Father John LeCornu, the prison chaplain, and Father Jones of the Walla Walla Catholic Church encouraged Quinn to confess and repent, but he resisted all efforts at religious counseling even though he had been a Baptist at one time. A number of clergymen tried to gain access to give religious advice, but Quinn refused them admittance and was rude and insulting to any clergyman who came near his cell. After word was received that the commutation had been denied, it fell upon Captain of the Guard J. D. Smith to tell him the news. When Smith advised the condemned man to "prepare for death with the break of day," Quinn paled at the news and became quite nervous. After Father LeCornu made his final plea to the prisoner to repent and confess, the priest reported, "That man will go to his death this morning refusing to embrace any salvation. When I talked with him he thinks he will 'die game.'"

Quinn seemed to have resigned himself to his fate, but he still had great difficulty sleeping that last night. After the prisoners were locked in their cells, the parts of the gallows were brought from storage and erected in the prison yard. Only carriage bolts and screws were used so no sound of a hammer could be heard, and none of the prisoners were disturbed. On the final day the prisoner was awakened at an early hour and ate a hearty breakfast before dressing in the black burial suit provided by the state. Before 5:00 a.m. Superintendent C. S. Reed arrived at his cell and read the death warrant and the record of appeals and respites, and then the procession formed. Quinn was escorted to the gallows by prison guards and the persistent clergymen. He faltered only slightly as he rounded the corner of the hospital building and saw the gallows for the first time. He climbed the thirteen stairs with a steady gait and, once upon the platform, stepped to the forward railing. He looked over the small crowd of witnesses, mostly physicians, prison officials, and newspaper reporters, and made a brief speech in which he continued to protest his innocence, still claiming that the shooting of his wife had been an accident. When he concluded he stepped backward onto the trapdoor, where his wrists and arms, knees and ankles were strapped, the black hood was pulled over his head, and the noose was carefully adjusted and cinched in place so it could not slip. In but a moment the lever was pulled and the trapdoor was sprung. Even though all was in the proper order and placement, Quinn failed to break his neck in the fall because the cords in the back of his neck were abnormally large. The prisoner slowly choked to death, and his legs began twitching. As he struggled he managed to loosen the straps on his arms, and he dropped them to the ground. Still gasping for breath, Quinn begged the officials, "This is awful, boys. For God's sake, take me up and drop me again, boys," but his pleas were ignored. Quinn struggled for some time as his speech became increasingly garbled and inarticulate, and finally he hung lifeless. Prison Dr. L. R. Quilliam monitored the prisoner's vital signs for twenty-two and one-half minutes before allowing the body to be cut down and placed in a coffin, and then the remains were turned over to Quinn's sister for burial.

Richard Quinn in prison
COURTESY OF WASHINGTON SECRETARY OF STATE

Prison officials warned the newspaper reporters that publication of the horrible details would result in prosecution under the public morals law. Newspapers that "printed the sickening details of the execution" violated a section of Oregon's criminal code that expressly forbid the publication of such matters, and the offense was punishable by "a fine of not more than $100."

On May 19, 1910, the *Spokane Daily Chronicle* announced that W. D. Dodd, the editor of the *Bellingham Herald,* had been arrested on information filed directly with the superior court charging a violation of the public morals statute forbidding the publication of the story of Richard Quinn's execution. Dodd asked for a speedy trial and was scheduled to appear on May 21, but no record of a conviction and fine has been found. An article in the *Walla Walla Union* newspaper was censored, leaving out all the gruesome details of the botched execution. It even showed a space in the text where the word "not" had been removed regarding Quinn's neck failing to break.

CHAPTER 20

An International Mass Murderer

In 1909 widow Agnes Jansen migrated from Germany to America, arriving in Spokane, Washington, in May and taking a room at the boardinghouse of Margaret Aherns. Three months later she met sixty-three-year-old James Logan—an alias as his real name was William Frederick Jahns—who had come to the city to hire a housekeeper. Jansen took the job and went with Logan to his Cedonia farm, where Logan employed two hired hands, George Hilton and Jack Tisth. In mid-October Logan went to Spokane and stopped by Aherns's boardinghouse to pick up Jansen's mail. She had received one letter written in German, but although Logan was German, he could not read the language. He had the letter translated and learned that his housekeeper had just received $3,500 in American money, which was to be transferred from a German bank to an American bank account in her name. Logan immediately began planning to murder his housekeeper and steal her money. He returned to his farm and began laying the groundwork.

Logan went to the abandoned Hergesheimer ranch and stacked a large pile of logs, six feet square and six feet high, to serve as a funeral pyre, and some logs were so large they had to be hauled by a horse. He then convinced Jansen to accompany him on a business trip to Chicago by telling her that he was going to recruit other Germans to settle on his extensive land holdings. On October 27, 1909, at about midnight, the couple left the Logan farm, but instead of turning toward Blue

Creek, where the train depot was located, Logan turned in the opposite direction toward the Hergesheimer ranch. Jansen, unfamiliar with the area, did not realize they were heading in the wrong direction. Three hours later they arrived at the gate to the Hergesheimer ranch, and Logan suggested they wait until daylight before continuing. Jansen agreed, and Logan jumped down from their wagon to open the gate so Jansen could drive the team through it. When Jansen came abreast of Logan, he suddenly pulled out his pistol and, without hesitation, shot her in the head twice. Logan dragged Jansen's body from the wagon, threw it on top of the huge stack of logs, and ignited the pyre. Within hours Jansen's remains were almost entirely consumed by the flames.

Logan had not expected anyone to be in the vicinity at that hour, but he was mistaken. He and Jansen were seen by Al Stayt as they pulled up to the Hergesheimer's gate. Later, the Giffords—Elmer, Ira, and their uncle Charles—were hunting in the area and saw the fire, which they knew was much too large for a mere campfire. The fire raised concern from other neighbors as well, and soon "Swede" Johnson came to investigate. Johnson did not have any reason to suspect foul play, so he left after a brief conversation with Logan. At 6:00 a.m. O. D. Taylor, a farmer living two miles from the Hergesheimer ranch, noticed the fire and also went to investigate. He found Logan asleep in his wagon. When aroused, Logan said that he had a sick horse so he had waited there while his housekeeper continued on to Blue Creek, riding with a man who had passed through during the night. As soon as the fire had burned down to a safe level and Logan felt certain Jansen's body had been entirely consumed in the flames, he turned around and continued on his way to Blue Creek, where he had claimed he was to meet Jansen. He arrived the next day, but he met a number of people along his route. He paid Johnny Cline to take his team and wagon back to Cedonia, and he went by train to Davenport. Once there, he went directly to the bank, identified himself as Jansen's husband, and tried to withdraw her money but was refused. Logan then took a room at a hotel and pondered about how to get his hands on Jansen's fortune.

After hunting throughout the night, the Giffords decided to investigate that huge fire they had seen, and they went to the Hergesheimer ranch. They picked through the ashes and found the remains of a human hand, so they hurried to Taylor's farmhouse to summon Stevens County Sheriff W. H. Graham from Colville. The sheriff arrived with coroner A. B. Cook and district attorney H. B. Kirkpatrick. During their investigation of the scene, they found a box of .32 caliber shells, a hat pin, wires from a woman's hat, a woman's belt buckle, corset stays, and a bit of bridgework. The ashes were carefully sifted, and the lawmen also found a small piece of a vertebrae, a piece of a skull, and a leg bone. Everything was documented and gathered for evidence, and they next documented the bloodstain at the gate and the wagon tracks in the muddy yard. The sheriff backtracked the wagon's route to the Logan farm, and Johnny Cline arrived with Logan's wagon while he was questioning the hired hands. Cline then told the sheriff that Logan had taken the train to Davenport, so Graham called Davenport Deputy Sheriff Gardiner to be on the lookout for Logan. The culprit was soon behind bars and gave up his .32 caliber Navy Colt revolver without resistance. Gardiner then searched Logan's room and found many incriminating items, including letters and checks belonging to a David R. Shively, who had been reported missing, and the letter in German addressed to Jansen. The Lincoln County sheriff also found a number of notary seals, stamps, and perforators used on railroads. Sheriff Graham went to Davenport and took custody of his prisoner and the evidence Gardiner had collected, and he believed he could solve a number of murder cases with this one arrest. He soon realized that Logan was not his prisoner's real name, so he sent copies of a photo around the region and had it published in the *Seattle Times* newspaper. From Bellingham deputy DeHaven

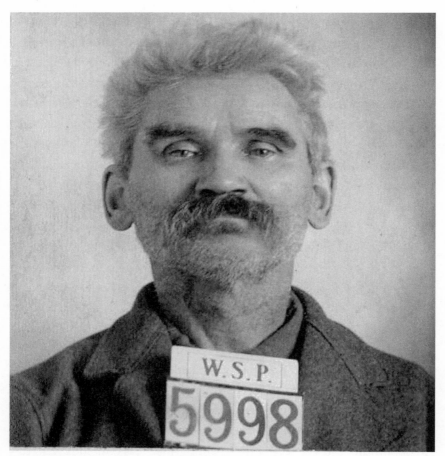

Serial killer William Frederick Jahns in prison
COURTESY OF WASHINGTON SECRETARY OF STATE

he learned Logan had previously used the name Romandorf and had disappeared from Maple Falls at the same time as James Logan. It was presumed Romandorf had assumed Logan's name to steal his property and money, but there was no direct evidence he had murdered Logan. It was also learned that soon after he began using the name Logan, he had lured Shively, a well-to-do landowner from Addy, to Spokane and poisoned him. He had stuffed the body into a trunk and shipped it to his Cedonia farm, where George Hilton buried it without questioning his order, or opening the trunk. George Hilton, it was then learned, was Logan's son Edward, and the photos of him circulated revealed he had been known in Maple Falls as Edward Romandorf.

During Logan's early days in jail, the story of his background began to unfold. When confronted with the developing information, Logan speculated, "I suppose that when you start trailing me back and find out I was once in South Africa, you will accuse me of doing things like that down there, too." This alerted Sheriff Graham that Logan, alias Romandorf, might have other aliases, so he sent photos to South Africa. He received a reply and learned Logan's true identity was William Frederick Jahns, sometimes misspelled Johns, and he was wanted for murdering eight men during diamond robberies. South African lawmen had tracked Jahns to New Orleans before losing his trail.

Jahns was indicted for the murder of Jansen, and his trial began on January 4, 1910, in Judge Daniel H. Carey's Colville courtroom. It took several days just to seat the jury before the district attorney presented a large number of witnesses whose testimony linked together a trail of evidence that seemed impossible to refute. The defense had elected not to plead insanity, but as the case against their client strengthened they decided to try that legal ploy. Unfortunately for the defense there were many reputable witnesses who were ready and able to refute their claim of insanity, and Drs. L. B. Harvey and M. F. Setter examined the defendant and pronounced him sane. When the jury retired to consider the evidence, they were out just one hour, long enough for two ballots, before bringing in a unanimous verdict of guilty of first-degree murder. Judge Carey then sentenced Jahns to hang at the prison in Walla Walla on April 21, 1911. He was delivered to the prison, registered as prisoner No. 5998, and lodged in the east wing of the cell block. Neither an appeal to the state supreme court nor the application for executive clemency to Governor Marion E. Hay delayed the fatal day.

Jahns was scheduled to hang at sunrise. The evening before his death, after the prisoners were locked in their cells, the parts of the gallows were brought from storage. The gallows was erected in the prison yard using carriage bolts and screws so no sound of a hammer could be heard, and neither the condemned man nor the other prisoners were disturbed. During his final days in prison, Jahns had spent his time reading everything he could acquire. As the days passed, officials were hopeful that Jahns would eventually confess to other crimes they suspected he had committed. They especially wanted him to give the location of the remains of the missing Logan and details related to the unsolved murder of a Bellingham butcher named Frederick L. Dames, but the prisoner would not speak of those men or any other crimes he may have committed. On the final morning the prisoner was awakened at an early hour and ate a hearty breakfast before dressing in the black burial suit provided by the state. Before 5:00 a.m. Superintendent C. S. Reed arrived at Jahns's cell in the east wing and read the death warrant, and then the procession formed. Jahns was escorted to the gallows, where he climbed the thirteen stairs with a steady gait and, once upon the platform, stepped to the forward railing. He looked over the small crowd of witnesses, mostly lawmen and newspaper reporters, and made a brief speech in which he argued his innocence. When he concluded he stepped backward onto the trapdoor and his wrists and arms and knees and ankles were strapped securely. The black hood was pulled over his head and the noose was adjusted and cinched tightly to keep it in place. In a moment the lever was pulled, the trapdoor was sprung, and Jahns dropped straight down, breaking his neck in the fall. Prison Dr. L. R. Quilliam was in attendance and he later announced that death was instantaneous, though he monitored vital signs for a brief period before pronouncing the prisoner dead. The body was then cut down, deposited in the coffin provided, and delivered to the dead man's son Edward Jahns, alias Romandorf and Hilton, for burial.

BIBLIOGRAPHY

Brown, Larry K. *You Are Respectfully Invited to Attend My Execution.*
    Glendo, WY: High Plains Press, 1997.

Gilbreath, West. *Death on the Gallows.* Silver City, NM: High-
    Lonesome Books, 2002.

Horan, James D., and Paul Sann. *Pictorial History of the Wild West.*
    New York: Bonanza Books, 1954.

McLoughlin, Dennis. *Wild and Woolly: An Encyclopedia of the Old
    West.* New York: Barnes & Noble Books, 1975.

Nash, Jay Robert. *Encyclopedia of Western Lawmen & Outlaws.* New
    York: Da Capo Press, 1994.

Thrapp, Dan L. *Encyclopedia of Frontier Biography, in Three Volumes.*
    Lincoln: University of Nebraska Press, 1988.

Wilson, R. Michael. *Crime & Punishment in Early Arizona.* Las
    Vegas: RaMA PRESS of Las Vegas, 2004.

———. *Murder & Execution in the Wild West.* Las Vegas: RaMA
    PRESS of Las Vegas, 2006.

CHAPTER 1: A SOLDIER'S REVENGE

Enterprise (Prescott, AZ), July 4, 1877, March 16, 1878.

Miner (Prescott, AZ), February 5, 1878, March 15–16, 1878, March
    22, 1878, June 11, 1880.

CHAPTER 2: "GOOD-BYE, BOYS!"

Cornish, Ken. "Mad Dog Dilda." *Old West* (Spring 1972): 16.

Kutac, C. "The Last Days of Dennis Dilda." *True West* (July 1994):
    18.

Boston Daily Globe, February 6, 1886.

Logansport (IN) *Pharos Tribune,* February 6, 1886.

Prescott (AZ) *Miner,* January 6, 1886, February 10, 1886.
Reno Evening Gazette, December 23, 1885.

CHAPTER 3: BETRAYAL OF A BENEFACTOR
Gillespie, L. Kay. *The Unforgiven, Utah's Executed Men.* Salt Lake
     City: Signature Books, 1991.
Daily Tribune (Salt Lake City, UT), August 12, 1887.
San Francisco Chronicle, August 12, 1887.

CHAPTER 4: "THE SHADOW OF DEATH HOVERING O'ER ME."
Helena (MT) *Independent,* August 8–10, 1889.
Inter-Mountain (Butte, MT), August 9, 1889.
Miner (Prescott, AZ), August 9, 1889.

CHAPTER 5: THE CARLISLE KID
Griffith, A. Kinney. "Mickey Free—Manhunter!" *Old West* (Fall
     1868): 2.
Hayes, Jess G. "Apache Vengeance." *Frontier Times* (August/September 1969): 10.
Arizona Citizen (Tucson, AZ), December 27, 1889.
Arizona Silver Belt (Globe, AZ), May 25, 1889, December 28, 1889.

CHAPTER 6: VIRGINIA CITY'S IRON BRIDGE GALLOWS
Los Angeles Herald, September 19, 1891.
Morning Call (San Francisco, CA), September 19, 1891.
News (Carson City, NV), September 20, 1891.
Record-Union (Sacramento, CA), November 5, 1891.
Reno Evening Gazette, July 6, 1891, September 19–20, 1891.
Tombstone (AZ) *Epitaph,* September 27, 1891.

CHAPTER 7: THE TRAMP MURDERER
Weekly Missoulian (Missoula, MT), December, 21, 1892.

CHAPTER 8: OVERCOME BY HIS LUST!

Churchs Ferry (ND) *Sun*, January 20, 1894.

Daily Globe (St Paul, MN), January 20, 1894.

Grand Forks (ND) *Daily Herald*, January 17–18, 1894, January 20, 1894.

San Francisco Chronicle, January 20, 1894.

CHAPTER 9: A DOUBLE TWITCH-UP IN CAÑON CITY

Rocky Mountain News (Denver, CO), December 5, 1894, May 10–12, 1895.

San Francisco Chronicle, May 12, 1895.

CHAPTER 10: A TRAIN ROBBERY IN COW CREEK CANYON

Meier, Gary, and Gloria Meier. *Oregon Outlaws.* Boise, ID: Tamarack Books, 1996.

Patterson, Richard. *The Train Robbery Era.* Boulder, CO: Pruett Publishing Company, 1991.

State of Oregon, prison records: Prisoner No. 1760, February 2, 1886; Prisoner No. 2293, January 2, 1892.

Astorian (Astoria, OR), November 16, 1889.

Oregonian (Portland, OR), November 15, 1889, July 2–3, 1895, December 24, 1895.

San Francisco Chronicle, January 30, 1897, May 25, 1897.

St. Louis Globe Democrat, July 1, 1895, July 3, 1895.

CHAPTER 11: JERKED TO JESUS!

Yaeger, Bill. *The Hanging of Billy Calder; the story of the only legal execution in Montana's Fergus County* (self-published pamphlet).

Butte (MT) *Miner*, March 17, 1900.

Fergus County Argus (Lewistown, MT), March 13, 1900, March 17, 1900, March 21, 1900.

Great Falls (MT) *Daily Tribune,* March 17–18, 1900.

Inter Mountain (Butte, MT), March 16, 1900.

CHAPTER 12: THEY KILLED THE CAPTAIN

Butte (MT) *Miner,* April 3–5, 1901.

Inter Mountain (Butte, MT), April 3–5, 1901, September 5–7, 1901.

CHAPTER 13: MURDER ON THE HIGH SEAS

Burlington (IA) *Hawk-eye,* August 30, 1903.

Hawaiian Gazette (Honolulu, HI), November 4, 1902, November 18, 1902, December 23, 1902, July 23, 1903, August 14, 1903, August 18, 1903, August 21, 1903.

Morning Leader (Port Townsend, WA), August 26, 1902, November 7, 1902, August 18, 1903.

Salt Lake Tribune (Salt Lake City, UT), July 8, 1903.

CHAPTER 14: EXECUTION BY FIRING SQUAD

Gillespie, L. Kay. *The Unforgiven, Utah's Executed Men.* Salt Lake City: Signature Books, 1991.

Salt Lake Tribune (Salt Lake City, UT), December 18–19, 1901, November 21, 1903.

CHAPTER 15: "I'LL GO TO HELL SURE."

Inter Mountain (Butte, MT), May 5, 1905.

Meagher (MT) *Republican,* December 2, 1904, December 9, 1904, December 23, 1904, March 24, 1905, March 31, 1905, April 28, 1905, May 5, 1905.

CHAPTER 16: THE BRUTAL MURDER OF AMANDA YOUNGBLOOD

Hunt, Robert V., Jr. "Not Fit to Die." *True West* (January 1992): 22.

Rocky Mountain News (Denver, CO), June 14–17, 1905.

Chapter 17: Carnage in the Desert

Carson City (NV) *Morning Appeal,* December 4, 1898.
Carson City (NV) *News,* December 14, 1899, September 8–9, 1905.
Los Angeles Herald, November 5, 1898, November 14, 1898.
San Francisco Call, November 30, 1898.
San Francisco Chronicle, December 2, 1898.

Chapter 18: Swift Justice in South Dakota

Aberdeen (SD) *American News,* June 25, 1909, July 6, 1909, November 16, 1909.

Chapter 19: The Wife Murderer

Everett (WA) *Herald,* September 23–24, 1908.
Everett (WA) *Tribune,* September 19, 1908, September 23, 1908, May 13–14, 1910.
Morning Union (Walla Walla, WA), May 13, 1910.
Spokane (WA) *Chronicle,* May 19, 1910.

Chapter 20: An International Mass Murderer

Bellingham (WA) *Herald,* April 21, 1911.
Idaho Statesman (Boise, ID), April 22, 1911.
Spokane (WA) *Review,* October 30–31, 1909, November 4–7, 1909, January 2–4, 1910, January 9, 1910, January 12–22, 1910, April 21–22, 1911.

Index

About the Author

R. Michael Wilson has been researching the Old West for twenty years, following a quarter century as a law enforcement officer. His particular interest is crime, and his writing philosophy is "the truth, the whole truth, and nothing but the truth."

Wilson served as a consultant for an episode of The History Channel's "Wild West Tech" and is an active member of the Wild West History Association (WWHA) and Western Writers of America (WWA).

Crime and punishment in America's early West is Wilson's area of interest and expertise. He is the author of *Great Stagecoach Robberies of the Old West, Great Train Robberies of the Old West, Frontier Justice in the Wild West, Tragic Jack: The True Story of Arizona Pioneer John William Swilling, Massacre at Wickenburg,* and *Outlaw Tales of Wyoming.* He lives in Las Vegas, Nevada, with his wife, Ursula.